# LOST
# PARISH CHURCHES
### OF
# ESSEX

## Andrew Barham

Ian Henry Publications

ISBN 0 86025 496 8

Dedication
I would like to dedicate this book to my wife, Andrea,
who, despite having her own books to write,
tirelessly helped me in the difficult job
of translating my research notes into English.
For her encouragement despite my talking endlessly
about churches for six years
and for her support in so many other ways.

The watercolour on the front cover is of Layer Breton old church
by Thomas Simpson
The photograph on the back is of Mistley Towers

Published by
Ian Henry Publications, Ltd.
20 Park Drive, Romford, Essex RM1 4LH
and printed by
Whitstable Litho Printers, Ltd.
Millstrood Road, Whitstable, Kent CT5 3PP

Acknowledgements

My thanks go to the staff of the Essex Record Office who directed me towards publications, documents, maps and pictures I would have otherwise never known existed. To Fred Whiffen for his tireless search for pictures of lost churches. To land owners in the county who kindly allowed me to take photos of their gardens and fields. Also to my wife, Andrea, and my friend, Ian Yearsley, who, as authors, inspired me both to start the book and to finish the project.

Sources

I am particularly indebted to a number of 18th and 19th century historians and writers whose work I drew from. Holman's parish notes of the early 18th century were used widely. As they were by Morant to construct his two Volumes of *Morant's Essex*. Published in 1768, they are a useful guide to the historical and genealogical description of each parish. H W King's *Essexiae Ecciesiasticae* (housed in the Essex Record Office) gives much-needed information on the state of Essex churches in the middle of the 19th century. I have drawn on his descriptions on many occasions. Wright's *Essex*, published in 1831, is another useful 19th century source. Buckler's *Twenty Two Churches of Essex* (1856) is a particularly useful book having chapters on four of 'my' churches. Benton's *History of the Rochford District*, published in the last few years of the 19th century, was used for descriptions of Little Stambridge and Shopland. Last, but certainly not least, the four volumes of the Royal Commission of Historical Monuments in Essex of the 1920s were an invaluable aid for those churches sadly lost during this century. A full bibliography is at the back of this book.

Fred Roe.

Shopland church porch
sketched in 1903

# Essex Churches

In the early 1990s, Ian and I set ourselves the task of visiting all the original parish churches of Essex. Our hobby turned into an obsession as we clocked up over 400 of these historical monuments - we put the list together from the Essex parish map produced by the Record Office. We spent almost two years completing our mammoth undertaking, which took us into corners of Essex that many local residents never visit - take a summer drive and start exploring the beautiful countryside of Essex.

Just as we thought we'd completed our task, we noticed that we'd left a number of parishes unvisited. Dotted around the county were parishes where there was no visible church: where had they once stood?

Sometimes the church building had been placed elsewhere in the parish but there were still traces of the original on the old site. The church of St Peter, Wickham Bishops, survives almost in its entirety while those of Steeple or Mistley have all but vanished with their foundations barely visible.

Then there were parishes who few people - other than interested locals - had even heard of, and which virtually died out with the passing of the parish church. Examples of these are Mose, Brundon and Snoreham.

Finding the sites of these former parish churches was easy in some cases and downright difficult in others. Most are not shown on modern maps and in many instances, not on old maps either. The Chapman and André maps of Essex of 1777 were invaluable in the early stages. (It was not until relatively recently that I discovered that some of the first and second editions of the Ordnance Survey map showed the precise sites of some of these lost churches!)

The more I found out, the more alive these churches became to me. The site of Virley is merely a ruin but when I found its description by Baring-Gould, it lived again in my imagination. Walton's church had fallen into the sea; Langenhoe was known as the Earthquake Church and the Saxon church of St Runwald's, Colchester, had some final humiliating years as the wall of a urinal before its eventual demolition.

I searched for a book on the lost parish churches of Essex but had to content myself with *Essex Churches; a wasting asset* by Warwick Rodwell in which he lists several demolished churches. I started researching in the Essex Record Office and found more lost churches but I wanted to find out everything. I compiled a comprehensive list so I could visit the site of every parish church that had ever stood in Essex!

Four years later, I was still coming across them (I have only learned about Little Barling in the past few months). I believe now that my list is complete. If you believe otherwise I'd be most interested to hear from you.

I suppose I began researching the book for purely selfish reasons. I enjoy the history, the architecture and the social impact of churches and I also wanted to find out why churches fell into decline. However, I soon realised that this interest was not unique to me. I don't profess to be an eminent historian or an accomplished archaeologist - I am a Computer Systems Analyst by profession - but I am a very enthusiastic local historian and a seasoned photographer. I owe to Ian and my wife, Andrea, the joy of the completion of this book which slowly came together over five absorbing years.

Which churches are included

My publisher and I were determined to make the book as definitive as possible. Churches lost through demolition were obvious candidates. But what about chapels, ruins or those converted into houses or used for secular purposes such as museums? Churches that had been substantially rebuilt such as Foulness, Childerditch and Widford were another category I needed to consider. The list was growing and I needed to define some parameters.

Eventually, after much deliberation, I decided to include only those that had been rebuilt on a different site such as at East Hanningfield, Woodham Walter and Layer Breton. I have added a list of churches and chapels that did not entirely qualify for inclusion such as those invested in the Church Conservation Trust (formerly the Redundant Churches Fund). There are possibly omissions but I have tried my best to limit these to the more obscure.

Reasons for demise

Essex has lost churches for many different reasons. It is believed that our first recorded lost church, Thunderley, was as a consequence of the Black Death in the 14th century. The population moved away from the church (or died) and it became ruinous.

In the majority of cases, when a parish church was located in an isolated position, with a dwindling population, it was often just not possible to generate the huge sums of money necessary to maintain it.

Some churches were lost to man-made or natural disasters. Fires, earthquakes, lightning strikes, erosion by the sea and Second World War bombing have all contributed. Vandalism too has taken its toll. Pitsea church was, until recently, crumbling on its hill overlooking the town. Vandals had hammered away at the floor and smashed all the windows. The tower was in danger of crashing down. Recently the nave and chancel was demolished to ensure no one was hurt by falling masonry.

Just a few years ago, this church was still used for regular worship. Vandalism, of course is not a 20th century affliction - there are many records of vandalism to churches from earlier generations.

Owners' privacy

If you wish to visit a site, write to the owners first to save a wasted journey. Remember, many sites are on private property and therefore not open to the public. Guy Harlings (see Appendix C) produces a publication that lists the names, addresses and telephone numbers of churchwardens. Churchwardens are often the best people to advise on contacting the site-owner.

What the future holds

Since I began my visits in the early 1990s, I have noticed a steady growth in churches becoming redundant or disused. When re-visiting some churches barely a year later, I'm saddened to see that some are no longer open to the public. There are, however, a number of institutions and charities dedicated to saving historic buildings: very often our parish churches. With contributions from the likes of you and me, they can be maintained. Let us hope that the new millennium will see these wonderful historic treasures with their futures assured. I have taken the liberty of listing the addresses of these worthy institutions in this book. Please consider joining one or more to help save our heritage.

Aldham church from an early 19th century sketch

Aldham
(OS Ref: TL 9067 2539)

Situated beside Church House Farm, the original parish church of Aldham lay almost a mile west of the present building. The church was dedicated to St Margaret and St Catherine: however, White's *Directory of Essex* of 1863 gives the honour to St Ann.

According to Morant the church consisted of "a body and south aisle; but the chancel is only of one pace; the whole tyled. On the west end of the church there is a small erection of timber, rough cast, and tyled containing two bells."

In 1818, *Excursions through Essex* added that "A ruinous old chapel on the north side of the church has been taken down many years; and there is nothing at present remarkable in the church." 1853 saw the old building in such a dilapidated state that the church authorities decided to demolish it and build a new one. A factor that added to this decision was the inconvenient location of the existing church. Thomas Burch Western donated "a certain piece of land containing one hundred and eighteen poles" in the centre of the village, for this purpose.

Certain conditions were attached to the rebuilding. The primary being that permission would not be given for demolition until sufficient funds were raised for the replacement building. The new church was to be as similar to the former as possible. The Essex Record Office houses plans of both the new and old churches, drawn up in December, 1853. Indeed, when the two are compared, they are virtually identical, with the exception of the large Victorian tower.

As much as possible of the original materials and features of the old church were incorporated into the new. Documents relating to rebuilding instructed: "Take down the whole of the present church, clean, cart and stack the material for use on the new site. Such materials only as good sound and fit for the purpose are to be rended - all else to be the property of the rector or churchwardens and to be left on the ground ... It is to be understood that the new church is to be built in exact accordance with the old church with such alterations and additions only as are specifically set forth in the drawings and referred to in the specification, it is therefore required that before the old church be pulled down the drawings are to be carefully compared there with and all the dimensions tested." Edward Hakewill was commissioned to build the new church. Its consecration ceremony took place on 13 July, 1855.

Thanks to these instructions, visitors to the present Victorian church can now view these incorporated features. Three 13th century windows were placed in the west wall of the south aisle. A 13th century south doorway was also placed in this aisle, along with a 14th century doorway in the north east corner. There is a 14th century window in the north vestry. The turret houses two small 14th century windows. In the chancel, there are three 15th century windows. The roofs of the chancel, nave and south aisle are 15th century. The beautifully carved 14th century porch was moved in its entirety to the new church and continues to grace the entrance today.

The two ancient bells were removed from the old church and now inhabit the new. The first bears the Latin inscription: "*Sum Rosa Pulsata Mundi Katerina Vocata*" and is dated about 1400. The second is inscribed: "*Sancta Margareta Ora Pro Nobis*" and is from the early 16th century.

Aldham had the renowned Essex historian, Philip Morant, as rector from 1745 until his death in 1770, when he was buried in the old churchyard. His monument lay on the site for almost a hundred years after the demolition of the old structure. In 1966, The Essex Archæological Society removed it to the interior of the new church where it can be seen today. The monument reads: "Beneath this stone are deposited the remains of the Reverend Philip Morant, A.M., 25 years rector of this parish, died November 25th 1770. Aged 70. Also, of Anne his wife, died July 28th 1767 aged 69."

There are no remains of the original structure on the old site. The approximate location can be determined by studying the sketch. A helpful way of determining the layout is by bearing in mind that the belfry was at the west end and the porch was on the south side. The Royal Commission described it as having been a building 72 feet long by 21 feet wide.

Location: The old church was sited next to Church House Farm, in Rectory Road, barely a mile or so north west of the A12. The land is now the property of Church House Farm. Please obtain permission from the owner before entering their land.

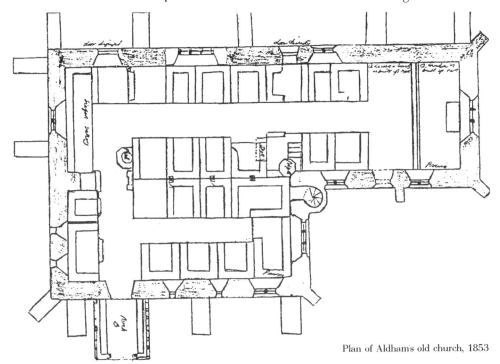

Plan of Aldham's old church, 1853

Alresford
(OS Ref: TM 0647 2066)

It is thought that the church of St Peter, Alresford, was originally built in the 10th or 11th century. It possibly contained an apsidal end at this time. The 14th century saw it completely rebuilt by Audrey (or Anfrey) de Staunton. In the chancel, a large stone was inscribed to this effect. The consequences of this rebuilding were a wider nave, resizing of the chancel and replacing of parts of the doors and windows.

The church consisted of nave, chancel, south aisle, south vestry and a north porch. At the west end, a low timber belfry with a shingled spire housed a single bell. Originally, two bells were present at the time of Morant and Wright.

The walls, built of rubble, were covered with cement and dressed with limestone. The chancel was 22 feet by 16 feet and described by the Royal Commission as having "no ancient features except a triangular headed opening in the east gable and part of the jambs of the window in the south wall which are of c.1300". The board outside tells us that "A small chancel arch was dominated by a large centrally placed pulpit... most of the windows were wooden frames replacing the early stone work." The nave was 39 feet by 21 feet and had a 14th century north doorway. Roman tiles can be seen in the north west corners. The roof of the nave had one old tie beam. The west gallery featured twisted balusters.

The 19th century found the church in a sorry state. The middle of the century saw much alteration to the structure. The chancel floor was raised, the chancel arch widened and most of the windows replaced. A new stone porch was added as was a south aisle (housing two 14th century windows) and a vestry. The roof was completely retiled and the bell turret replaced.

However, disaster struck at midnight on 1 October, 1971, when a huge fire engulfed the church. The cause of the fire remains unclear - some are adamant that it was an arsonist. The roof was completely destroyed, as were all the windows. Nothing remained except the walls and porch. Funds were not available to rebuild the church. St Andrew's, a newly built church was opened in March, 1976, and parishioners now worship within this new structure.

By 1977, the remains of St Peter's Church were all but demolished. The ruins were prey to vandals and adventurers. Since the church council was responsible for the site, they resolved to raze it to the ground, fearing claims for injury. The Rector was recorded as saying, "Of course if someone would work a miracle and provide means or money to make the building safe, I should be delighted to urge the PCC to reconsider its position." Essex County Council gallantly provided funds with which to make the ruin safe, spending £1,500 to make the tops of the walls sound. Today, the ruins still stand for the interested observer to visit.

Location: The church is just south of the village of Alresford. Take Church Road south towards the Ford - this road becomes Ford Lane. The ruins of the church are about halfway down this lane on the right-hand side of the road.

Alresford church, c.1969

Ruins of Alresford church

## Belchamp St Ethelbert
## (OS Ref: TL 8052 4326)

Llittle is known about Belchamp St Ethelbert, beyond its approximate site, which now lies under ploughed land. Morant states that "Beauchamp St Ethelbert is part of the parish of Ovington but was anciently distinct." Warwick Rodwell however puts it firmly (and in my view correctly) in the parish of Belchamp Otten (whose church is St Ethelbert and All Saints).

The two parishes have been united since 1473 and the chapel, dedicated to St Ethelbert, sometimes called St Albright, was possibly demolished or left to ruins at this time. Whether any of the materials from this church were incorporated into the churches of Ovington or Belchamp Otten is uncertain but very likely. This practice was often the case on the demise of unused or unwanted churches.

According to Thomas Wright (1836), by 1650 the parliamentary survey reported that the chapel had been "long since down."

Unfortunately, nothing is known of its appearance or age. However, Roman bricks and quern fragments have been found on the site in recent years. Little of the original stone has been recovered. Today the observer can discern nothing of the ancient structure from the site. In fact, it is difficult to tell with any certainty in which field the actual site was.

Location: Nothing remains of the church at the above OS Reference which is in the middle of a field on private property. It's not really worth the visit unless you are a real enthusiast.

Belchamp Otten church

Berners Roding
(OS Ref: TL 6021 1005)

This church, 7 miles from Ongar, has no known dedication - if most sources are to be believed. However, I have recently found that the publication by the Essex Record Office *A Genealogist's Guide to the ERO* states the dedication as All Saints. The name of the parish derives from its mediæval benefactors, the Berners family, who hailed from the town of Berniers in Normandy.

The majority of the building dates from the 14th century. It was subject to many additions and alterations over the next five centuries.

Morant describes the church as "a small edifice, tyled, near the Hall; and the chancel is ruinous, unless it hath been lately repaired. A mean wooden turret contains 1 bell."

On the whole, Morant's description of the church is still applicable today. The walls are of flint-rubble and red brick, dressed with limestone, clunch and then more brick. The chancel is 20.5 feet by 17 feet with a 16th century east wall and a 16th century east window. There is a 14th century blocked doorway in the south wall. Unusually, there is no chancel arch; 16th century brick piers support the beam across the chancel. Remains of a 14th century piscina can be seen here.

The nave was 37.5 feet x 19 feet, although this appears to have been shortened during this century. Comparisons between a turn-of-the-century photograph of the old church and the present day structure show that not only has the church lost its small wooden belfry but the western end of the nave appears to have lost a few feet in length.

Berners (pronounced "Barnish") Roding church has a 15th century blocked north doorway. The 16th century brick porch was partly rebuilt in about 1800. There are two windows in the south wall: one from the 16th century and a more modern example. There are two 14th century windows. The east window dates to the 16th century. Buttresses were added in the 18th and 19th centuries in an attempt to shore up the walls.

The roofs of the chancel and nave are 16th century.

The lone bell, fashioned by John Dyer in 1594, has vanished. Presumably, it was removed when the bell turret was taken down and the west end was shored up. Hopefully it has found another home at a nearby church. Other lost artifacts include a plate dated 1627 and the monuments to Thomas Carowe of 1591 and, Joan, his wife, of 1593. The church registers date from 1590.

By 1763, services were being held just once a month, due to the dwindling local population. Over the next two centuries the fabric of the church crumbled and decayed. At the time of the Royal Commission survey (c. 1920) the condition of the church was described as "poor, bad cracks in the walls and buttresses [are] falling away."

Finally, on 13 December, 1957, the parish of Berners Roding was united with that of Shellow Bowells and the Willingales. The poor condition persists today; the church is in an advanced state of decay at present. No doubt it would take many thousands of pounds to repair.

In a recent summer, Berners Roding had a lone occupant in the form of a barn owl. Only determined visitors will be prepared to negotiate past the heap of droppings and brave the attentions of an angry bird.

Location: From Chelmsford take the A1060 north west. Just before reaching Margaret Roding, take a left-hand turn towards the Willingales. About a mile south, take another left-hand turn towards Berners Hall. The church is next to the Hall. The key is available from the farm next door.

Tudor south window, Berners Roding

Interior of Berners Roding church, 1995

11

Berners Roding church, with timber belfry (now demolished), c.1900 (*reproduced with the permission of Essex Record Office*)

The site of Brundon church, 1997

Brundon
(OS Ref: TL 8540 4165)

Brundon church has been lost for many centuries. No one knows exactly when it was demolished, although it is thought to have happened in the 17th century. Its layout and dimensions are a mystery. Our only clue to its appearance lies in the fact that it was thought to be small.

Brundon church was combined with the parish of Ballingdon many years ago. In 1863, Ballingdon-cum-Brundon was described as having 813 acres and 861 inhabitants. This was in turn annexed, in the 1830s, to the Borough of Sudbury. The ruins were still visible in the time of Morant [1765]. "The remains of it are in a little enclosure, about a mile on the left hand of Ballingdon Street, directly opposite to Borley church." It is also described as being "close to Brundon Wood."

Thomas Wright, writing in the 1830s, says: that it had been "entirely demolished a long time ago". In 1863, White's *Directory of Essex* states that "Its ancient church, which stood at Brundon ... went to decay many years ago and no traces of it are now extant."

Today, nothing remains of the church ruin on the site, save a few pieces of red tile scattered across its former site, now a ploughed field.

A folly in the garden of a house in Newton Street, Sudbury, contains stone and brick work from an earlier structure, probably this ancient church.

Location: The church was situated at the above grid reference. Refer to the point marked on the accompanying map. In my opinion, the church lay to the north of the hedge, on the bend of the footpath.

The site of Brundon church (*reproduced from the 1879 Ordnance Survey map*)

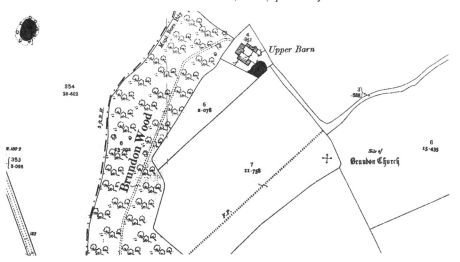

13

Folly in Sudbury, containing stone
from Brundon church

Site of Chignall St Mary church,
showing surrounding moat

Chignal St Mary
(OS Ref: TL 6655 1070)

At the top of a hill, a mile north of the church of Chignal St James, stood the church of Chignal St Mary sometimes referred to as Chignal or Chicknall Tany.

The parishes of Chignal St James and St Mary were probably merged around 1360. This indicates that St Mary's was already deteriorating and was allowed to deteriorate further. It has been speculated that this building may have been the original Saxon of wood and stone, reconstructed in the 12th and 13th centuries. Its size and proportions are not known.

The reason for demolishing Chignal St Mary is unclear. Perhaps it was due to dwindling receipts from too few parishioners, or the proximity of two other churches: Chignal St James and Chignal Smealey. According to Pusey in *A Discovery of Old Essex*, the three parishes of Smealey, St James and St Mary were merged into one in 1888.

A useful amount of information on the site of the church exists. Morant's 18th century account runs as follows: "For there is a field of the Glebe, called St Mary's croft, in which a parcel of land, about the bigness of a church-yard, is inclosed with a bank and deep ditches on all sides, except the west and some ruins of a building have been ploughed up, bricks and stones still remaining scattered about or lately did so."

Wright mentions the 'croft' on which the church was situated. "Belonging to the glebe there is a small field, called St Mary's croft, which was formerly the church-yard belonging to the church of St Mary."

The church was described as being almost opposite the school and schoolhouse, two-thirds of a mile north of the church of St James. Cottages occupied the site for many years until they were demolished. In 1931, a house named 'St Mary's Croft', was erected on the site. One side of the moat still exists. In recent years, a couple of fragments of stones have been unearthed in the gardens of the current occupants.

Location: The church was on land that now contains the house and gardens of St Mary's Cottage, on the road connecting Chignal St James with Chignal Smealy (near Chignal Hall). The land is private and, although the present owners are interested in the site and history of the church, they are unlikely to welcome too many unannounced enthusiasts trampling over their lovely gardens.

Colchester St Mary Magdalen
(OS Ref: TM 0059 2480)

The church of St Mary Magdalen stood at the junction of Magdalen Street and Brook Street. Recently demolished, the site has now become a sheltered housing complex. St Mary Magdalen's parish was the smallest in Colchester, consisting of barely fifty acres of land. The first building on or near the site, was a hospital. This included a chapel dedicated to St Mary Magdalen founded by command of Henry I "for the reception of leprous and infirm people: besides other endowments". It was given the tithes of St John's Abbey, which were distributed to the poor, in the form of bread, beer and meat.

In Edward VI's reign, St Mary's chapel was demolished. However, in 1610 the institution was refounded by James I under the title of "The College or Hospital of King James" The inhabitants consisted of a master and five paupers. The master "should have the cure of the souls of the parishioners of St Mary Magdalen, and pay each of the said five poor persons fifty-two shillings a year."

Morant describes this second building as "a very small building of one pace tyled. The little chancel is modern, and built of brick. In the wooden turret, at the west end there is one bell. The west end and turret, were damaged by Lightening in the year 1739, but have been since repaired." An engraving published in 1783 shows this building.

This was demolished in 1854 when it was replaced, a little to the south, by a Victorian church. Rodwell believed that the previous church was probably at the position of the "northernmost end of the present graveyard." There was no evidence of the previous church in the 1970s and there is certainly none since the later church was demolished. (The Almshouses in Brick Street represent the later foundation).

The replacement church included a small polygonal south-west turret, similar to that of Little Dunmow. Rodwell described it as "a drab building with little historic interest; it is found with knapped flints on a brick and rubble core (probably containing much mediæval stonework from the hospital). The facing flints are falling away at the east end and the soft limestone dressings around the windows and doorways are badly decayed. The cost of maintaining this building is great."

Indeed this was true. On 23 January, 1995, the latest church of that name was demolished after laying dormant for a number of years. Sadly, the local Family History Society was not informed so was unable to make full monumental transcriptions before the gravestones were destroyed.

Location: The church was sited on the corner of Magdalen Street and Brook Street. Remains of the buildings are no longer visible since sheltered accommodation has now been erected on the site.

St Mary Magdalen's old church, Colchester, 1783
St Mary Magdalen's replacement church, c.1910

St Mary Magdalene Church, Colches

17

Colchester St Nicholas
(OS Ref: TL 9978 2519)

The parish church of St Nicholas stood on the south side of Colchester High Street where now stands a large Co-op building. Possibly, a Saxon church occupied the site formerly. This was replaced in the 12th century and then entirely rebuilt in the 14th century.

At this stage of development, the church consisted of a chancel and north vestry, north and south transepts, and a nave with north and south aisles. A south chapel also existed, as did a north tower. The walls were a mixture of rubble and dressed with limestone.

In 1514, possibly due to falling attendances, a proposal was made to unite St Nicholas with the nearby parish church of St Mary's. However, this did not come about. In August, 1700, during much needed restoration, the tower tumbled into the nave, bringing the building to near total ruin. Fortunately, the workmen were at lunch at the time, so no one was injured. In 1721, the west end was repaired at a cost of £68 so that services could recommence.

In 1729, a timbered belfry was erected. According to Morant in the 1760s the nave was tiled and the south aisle was leaded. The tower was standing "about the middle of the body of the church, being partly built on the North wall. In it are Five bells and a clock with a dial projecting out into the street which occasions this to be vulgarly called the Dial-church. On the top of the Tower there is a small bell in a lantern, for the clock."

In 1870 the parish of St Nicholas was finally combined with another church, that of St Runwald. The latter was already earmarked for demolition at a later date. (See page 22). A bell made by Miles Graye in 1621 was taken from this condemned church to join the other five in St Nicholas. It also gained an early 18th century altarpiece painting of Christ. This painting has been recently sold at auction.

In the period 1875-6 St Nicholas was completely restored by Sir Gilbert Scott at a cost of £15,000. The chancel was largely rebuilt. The south aisle and transept chapel were destroyed and a new church of a much larger size was added to the south of the old building. The north tower was refaced and partly rebuilt and a spire was added. In 1905, the projecting clock was taken down.

The chancel was 25 feet by 15.5 feet and had a late 14th century piscina. There was a 14th century doorway. The crossing of the old church (14 feet by 15.5 feet) had early 14th century arches on each side. The nave was 27 feet by 18 feet and had an early 14th century north arcade. The north aisle was 11.5 feet wide.

In Worley's 1915 book on Essex churches, he describes St Nicholas as a "very fine building in the Decorated style ... The spire is nearly 150 feet in height. Though the fabric itself is new, care has been taken to preserve some interesting features from the old church." A new reredos, made by Temple Moore in about 1925, was installed.

St Nicholas Colchester. Street scene from early 19th century

Rear of St Nicholas, Colchester

After the Second World War, notices were served on St Nicholas for demolition. Despite numerous protests, it was eventually sold for £80,000. Demolition began in October, 1954, and the new Co-op building was completed in 1957.

Four bells from St Nicholas have recently been installed in Basildon.

Location: St Nicholas was sited on the corner of St Nicholas Street and Colchester High Street where the Co-operative store now stands. There are a few gravestones behind the store, but there are no visible remains of the structure.

St Nicholas, 1824

Colchester St Runwald
(OS Ref: TL 9963 2521)

St Runwald's stood in the middle of Colchester High Street, beside the Moot Hall (replaced by the current Town Hall in 1899). It had the distinction of being the only church in Essex, possibly England, dedicated to this saint. Rodwell, in his book *Historic Churches - A Wasting Asset*, suggests "The proportions of the building, the thickness of its walls and the dedication, would all accord well with a foundation of the later Anglo-Saxon period." The church also contained many interesting Norman features although the earliest documentary evidence dates back to only 1296.

Consisting of a nave, chancel, north aisle and vestry, the walls of this building were nearly 3 feet thick. The chancel was 17 feet by 15 feet. Its only means of light was the east window, which Buckler in 1856 simply described as "modern." The chancel had two fine Perpendicular Gothic arches that led into the north aisle. There has been some speculation that a chapel adjoined the chancel at one time, however no evidence of this existed in the 19th century. The nave was 30 feet by 17 feet and had one small dormer window in the north wall and a modem window in the west wall. There was also a west gallery in the nave. The pulpit was situated against the south wall. An ancient Norman doorway and oak door were on the south side.

The 15th century aisle was 27½ feet by 8½ feet and dedicated to St Mary Buckler described it as "a remarkably fine specimen of Perpendicular architecture." The aisle contained three triple-light windows in the north wall "with good tracery of uniform design, and carefully finished." The vestry was built in the Victorian period. The floor of the church was paved with stone and brick. A single bell resided in St Runwald's belfry, made in 1621 by Miles Graye.

St Runwald's appears to have sustained much damage during the 1648 Siege of Colchester, particularly to the chancel arch. Little was done to repair this damage at the time. The original spire was taken down in 1692 and replaced by a small wooden turret. In 1760, the church, having stood unused for a hundred years, was finally repaired. A new pulpit, pews and other church furniture were installed. At the time of this restoration, circular headed windows were adopted in accordance with the taste of that particular century.

In 1844, it was proposed that the parishes of St Runwald and St Nicholas should be combined and the latter church rebuilt. The plans for the new St Nicholas were submitted in 1851 but not approved. However, in 1873 the parishes were finally united. This spelt the end for St Runwald's: its final indignation being a short spell as the wall of the public urinal!

The demolition of St Runwald's began on 6 April, 1878. Photographs of its destruction are housed in the Holly Trees Museum, Colchester. The arches and columns dividing the chancel and north chapel were re-erected in St Albright's church, Stanway, during restoration there in 1879. St Runwald's 15th century octagonal font, described by Pevsner as "quite unusually interesting" was given to Little Totham parish church where it still resides.

The mural monument and the communion plate are both mentioned in earlier publications and were moved to St Nicholas on the demolition of St Runwald's. Their fate after this church was subsequently demolished in the 1950s is uncertain. The parish chest went to the Colchester Museum. The small graveyard associated with this church maintains its original position in West Stockwell Street.

It could be argued that St Runwald's church wasn't grand or particularly attractive. However, it is a great shame that a church with many unique features and of Saxon origin should have been so badly treated. On its former site in Colchester High Street, there is no monument to its passing. It has been replaced by a bus stop. As Rodwell pointed out "the site of St Runwald's is forgotten but is still there, under the road, and in all probability its foundations survive in part." Let us hope that one day archæological investigations unearth more of its origins.

Location: St Runwald's was near the corner of Colchester High Street and West Stockwell Street. This is now the home of a bus lay-by. The few remaining graves attached to the church can be viewed at the corner of West Stockwell Street and St Runwald's Street.

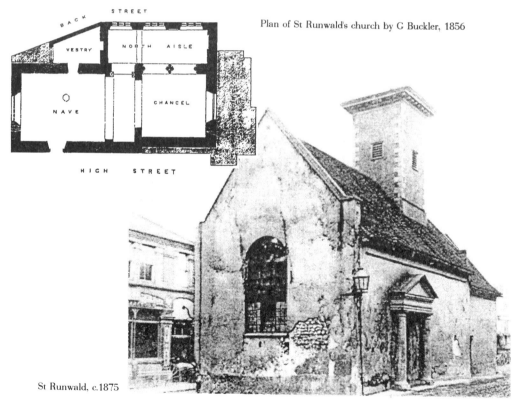

Plan of St Runwald's church by G Buckler, 1856

St Runwald, c.1875

St Runwald, photograph taken from St Nicholas, 1877

East Donyland old churchyard

# East Donyland
## (OS Ref: TM 0243 2120)

St Laurence, East Donyland, was demolished in 1838. At the same time, a new church was built in a place more properly known as Rowhedge. The original building stood to the left of the Colchester to Fingringhoe road, near the Hall and about three quarters of a mile from its replacement. It was a simple two-celled structure comprising a nave and chancel, with a west end bell turret. The sole survivors from the interior of the old church are two floor memorial slabs. In the old churchyard, some impressive monuments still exist; two of particular note from the 18th century. The exact outline of the church, however, is hard to discern.

As a consequence of an archæological dig in 1926, Reverend G Montague Benton gauged the dimensions of the church as approximately 38 feet x 20 feet. His excavations were hindered by numerous later burials on the site. He points out that these dimensions match those of the neighbouring Norman church of Fingringhoe. He maintained that the similarity in age, dimensions and style were significant.

In 1927, Benton described the church's appearance, drawing from information contained in a sketch by Captain Sanders dating from 1801. He states "The nave had on the south side a large window, apparently of two lights, and a small window, also of two lights with a dormer window immediately above; the two latter were probably inserted to light a ringing chamber or west gallery. Both nave and chancel had south doors..." The west porch and bell turret were obviously 18th century additions.

A tower must have been present on the original building since it was described as "redy to fall down" in 1610. It appears to have collapsed in the 17th century and been replaced by the bell turret, housing a single bell. Sanders sketch showed this feature.

In the visitation of 1633, a list of necessary reparations was recorded. The steeple needed boarding "on the top", the belfry door "is very rotten", the church "wants glazinge", the "chancell wants tylinge," the "chancell floor wants pavinge and reayringe" and the "chancell wants whitinge"

In 1684, a visitation again listed that the church needed 'whiting' and that the pavement needed repairing. Was this still outstanding from fifty-one years before? Well, yet again in 1707 it was ordered that "The Chancell be new and whited, the floor, the tileing repaired and the eves lathed and plastered". It is obvious from these reports that the parishioners could not afford the repairs necessary for the upkeep of the church.

St Lawrence was finally demolished in 1838. Perhaps this was due to its inconvenient situation; it lay more than a mile from Rowhedge where most of the population now lived. It had also become too small to house the growing congregation. No doubt, financial considerations also favoured replacement rather than repair.

Reverend V McGie Torriano set up a subscription to build the replacement. On 3 October, 1837, the foundation stone was laid. The new church was completed the

24

following year at a total cost of around £2,000.

The new structure made a radical departure from the original church design. Octagonal in shape and made of white brick, the design was based on the Chapter House of York Minster.

The original 15th century octagonal font was preserved and purchased for St Leonard's Church, Colchester. The bell was stolen from the old church in 1834. It is believed to have firstly been sunk in Mill Creek and then spirited off to the West of England to be sold.

Some fine brasses and a monument were re-housed in the new church. One brass depicts Nicholas Marshall in prayer dated 1621 and another is to his mother, Mary Graye, of 1627. A superb alabaster monument is dedicated to Elizabeth Marshall dated 1613.

Location: From Colchester drive towards Rowhedge. Pass through the village. Prior to the turning to East Donyland Hall, on the left is the old cemetery of East Donyland Church. The church was in the churchyard at the front of the cemetery, near the road. The west end with the belfry was situated quite near the existing gate, beside the main road. There are some interesting 18th century graves still to be seen.

East Donyland Church - Essex.

Sketch of East Donyland church by Captain Sanders, 1801

# East Hanningfield

(OS Ref: TQ 7665 9990)

The original All Saints church was sited behind the Hall about a mile south-west of the present village centre. It stood on this site for upwards of 600 years until disaster struck in the late 19th century.

The chancel was 23 feet by 17½ feet, built in the early 16th century of red brick. It had two brick windows in the south wall. The nave was 41 feet by 22½ feet and built in the 13th century or earlier of pudding stone and pebble-rubble. The north aisle was built in the 16th century and was 13 feet 3 inches wide. A 15th century piscina was sited in the chancel.

Morant described the church as consisting "of a body and a chancel both tyled. The steeple, containing 4 bells, is only a boarded frame standing on the west end, with a shingled shaft. At the north side of the church and part of the chancel, is a chapel or chantry built [in] brick." He also describes in some detail the painted glass in the south and west windows.

On 30 December, 1883, at about one o'clock in the afternoon, some time after the Sunday morning service, a fire broke out. The doors were locked. With nobody able to gain entrance, the fire spread rapidly. An elderly local was immediately sent to Chelmsford to raise the alarm with the fire brigade.

Parts of the roof fell in and the wooden furniture quickly ignited. Soon after the fire began, a bystander broke a window and a young lad was persuaded to climb into the burning building. Not only did he re-emerge; he managed to save the plate and some clerical garments. The firemen took just under an hour to arrive. By this time, there was little they could do. They simply stood by and watched the sad spectacle. One braved the flames to save the 16th century stained glass from the east window. The building continued to burn for the rest of the day and throughout the night.

The communion table was allegedly recovered from the flames - quite how is not known. Thankfully, a double disaster was averted as the parish registers dating from 1540 were at the rectory at the time.

The fire was thought to have begun in either the roof or the steeple. Some young boys were accused of striking matches near the church - an accusation they strenuously denied. Others believed that the fire started from the burner in the nave. No definite cause was ever fixed upon.

On first sight, the fire appears to have been an unmitigated disaster. However, a wonderful find emerged as a consequence of the blaze. It revealed some magnificent 13th century wall paintings, hidden behind the plaster for hundreds of years. They depicted Adam with his spade, Eve with her spindle and St Katherine of Alexandria with her wheel. Sacrifices of Cain and Abel and the death of Abel were also shown.

The Rector had a glass case made to protect these historic wall paintings. Vandals subsequently destroyed the case so for many years the painting was exposed to the

East Hanningfield old church, c.1920

Site of East Hanningfield old church today

open sky in the ivied ruins of the nave. In 1933 the expert, Professor Tristram removed a portion of these paintings from the wall for preservation. He made detailed drawings of those paintings that could not be satisfactorily removed. These rare examples of mediæval church paintings are now preserved in the Victoria & Albert Museum.

The church had been insured for £1,000. The money was used, not to restore the old, but to build a new church nearer the new centre of the community, at East Hanningfield Tye. This new church was built in a remarkably short time. Work began on 16 July, 1884, and it was consecrated less than a year later on 16 June, 1885.

The shell of the old church was left to stand as a ruin, with the exception of the chancel. This was repaired for use as a mortuary chapel some years later. The ruins of All Saints were left open to the elements for many years until they underwent a partial demolition in the 1930s.

The rest was demolished at a later date. The site is now farmland and inaccessible to the casual passer-by.

H W King learnt of the destruction of All Saints whilst transcribing Holman's parish notes. This caused him to record with dismay "Alas? before I have seen it." He'd had a visit planned. He gives a description of the memorials and inscriptions as recorded by Holman in the early 18th century. I sympathise with King. I too would have loved to have seen this church. Even the ruin, in all its glory, would have sufficed. Just a few graves remain in what is now a copse. With the help of old photos, it is just possible to discern where the original church was sited.

Location: Take the A130 from Chelmsford. About 2 miles south of the Howe Green roundabout turn left down Pan Lane. Head east for about a mile, then take the next right turn towards East Hanningfield Hall. The church was situated just behind this hall. A public footpath skirts the site. Nothing of the building remains to be seen. A handful of graves reside in a thicket. Check with the owners of the Hall before visiting the site.

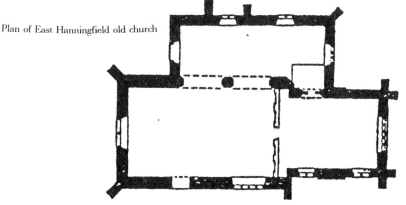

Plan of East Hanningfield old church

Great Warley
(OS Ref: TO 5965 8844)

The old church of St Mary the Virgin was to the south of Great Warley Hall. Holman described it in the early 1700s as being "situated on the left hand side of the road that leads to South Ockendon. The steeple was burnt down by lightning and had 5 bells in it. A tower of wood shingled with a shaft of one square piece of wood. 3 bells."

Holman goes on to describe many monuments and grave slabs in the chancel of the church. These included one to Margaret, wife of John Agmondesham, who died in 1582. The majority of the others were 17th and 18th century memorial slabs.

Morant confirms Holman's description: "On the top there is a small spire, of one square piece of wood." Wright describes the building simply as "an ancient building of brick." A north gallery was also present and the Arms of the Commonwealth (which rarely survived) were hung on the wall. In 1803, repairs were necessary to the tower and church walls. In 1833, the Rector's wife added a west gallery to join one situated on the north side.

S S Teulon redesigned the church in 1858 at a cost of £1,000. The chancel was rebuilt in yellow brick and the old west tower was demolished and rebuilt in red brick. A north vestry was added and the west gallery renewed. It could now accommodate 180 people. (Parts of the base of this later tower are still visible today, in the undergrowth.)

However, the popularity of this rebuilt church was not to last for long. The parish population had moved away from the Hall, up the hill towards Brentwood; the distance they had to travel to the church began to become a nuisance.

Most services in St Mary's church ceased in about 1892. At this time, a wooden mission church was built in the grounds of Fairstead, nearer to the new centre of the village, for the use of the parishioners. By 1910, Worley described the old church as "...now disused, except for funerals. It is a brick building of no particular interest and its nine 'little toy bells' are said to be dismally out of tune."

A new parish church was erected in 1904 and superseded the old church for services. It was designed by C Harrison Townsend and furnished by William Reynolds-Stephens in the Art Nouveau style. It was described as a "truly noble offering to God." This new church has gained a large amount of critical acclaim and is a fine example of its type.

Most of the former church of St Mary's was pulled down in the 1920s. The west tower survived until about 1966, then this too was demolished. On the site today gravestones are scattered over the wooded site. Many more are lined up against a brick wall. These include a few from the 18th century displaying the standard cherubs and skulls. The approximate site of the church can be divined from some brick and stone, which appear to be remains from the tower and part of the north wall.

Location: The site of the original church is a few hundred yards south of the A127, just to the south of Great Warley Hall. The land is kept by the owner of the Hall. Since it is walled off from the garden, visits to the site are permitted at any reasonable time.

Sketch of Great Warley's original church, c.1800
St Mary's, Great Warley, after restoration c.1900 (*reproduced with the permission of Essex Record Office*)

Hatfield Peverel
(OS Ref: TL 782 121)

The original parish church of Hatfield Peverel has been lost in the mists of time. Like the portion of the Priory church which, for the past few hundreds of years, has been used as the Parish church, it was possibly dedicated to St Andrew.

The original church probably fell into disuse and ruin some time between 1200 and 1550. Why this happened is uncertain, but it may be connected with the Priory burning down in 1231. The local parishioners were probably asked to contribute to rebuilding and subsequently permitted to worship there as a consequence of their donations. Since the Priory church was more accessible to locals, it probably became more popular. It is true to say that the Priory church was used for worship from about this time onwards and was still clearly in use at the time of the Dissolution of the Monasteries.

The site of the original church is thought to have been south-west of Hatfield Peverel railway station. The structure may have stood just to the south of 'Church Hills' field. Wright tells us that "The old church belonging to this parish formerly stood upon an eminence near the river, in a field between Hatfield-Bury and Terling called Church fields."

Although no evidence of the building remains, in 1952 some mediæval masonry was found at this location, near the mound, more or less where the river now runs.

In his book *A History of the Priory and Parish Church of St Andrew, Hatfield Peverel*, A J Steele tells us of an oil painting featuring the original church painted in about 1770. Presumably, as he puts it, this was an 'imaginary reconstruction' as there are no records of any structure being visible at this time. Neither is its site shown on the Chapman and André map of 1777. Steele says that the painting was given to the church by Mrs Arkwright in 1919 and now hangs in the upper vestry.

Location: The site is just north of the Chelmsford to Colchester railway line, in or near the field known as 'Church Hills'.

Hazeleigh
(OS Ref: TL 8359 0382)

The little church of St Nicholas, Hazeleigh, lay two and a half miles south-west of Maldon, next to the Old Hall. It has the dubious distinction of having often been quoted as 'the meanest church in Essex'. Made of lath and plaster over a timber frame it is thought to have been built by Giles Aleyne and his wife Sarah in about 1600. However, some authors have suggested that the chancel was built earlier while others believe the nave was built a century later. It is thought, by most historians, to have incorporated timbers from an earlier structure on the same site. The first rector was installed in 1390 before which Hazeleigh was only a chapel, perhaps attached to Woodham Mortimer church. Hazeleigh parish registers date from 1575.

It consisted of a nave, chancel, south porch and north vestry. The nave was 25 feet 6 inches by 17 feet 9 inches and had two original windows in the north wall, "each of three lights in a square head with moulded frames and mullions." There were also two windows in the south wall although the RCHM did not mention these. There was a small timber bell turret at the west end of the nave housing a single bell. The chancel was 11½ feet by 13 feet 3 inches and had a wooden, undecorated east window. The vestry (described by some as a 'lean-to') was 8 feet 3 inches by 11 feet 7 inches. The roofs were described by the RCHM as "ceiled and have principals with curved braces; the purlins of the chancel have carved side braces."

Fitch wrote in *Maldon and the Blackwater* that "Almost the only noteworthy feature is the 16th century hour-glass stand projecting from the wall close by the crooked and irregularly shaped reading desk, which is dominated by a distorted pulpit with a skimpy sounding board." The *Essex Review* states "The whole of the window frames were wooden and appear to have been just ordinary cottage casements, two small ones in the porch, and two on both the north and south sides and one in the east".

In 1684, the Venerable Thomas Turner, Archdeacon of Essex, paid the church a visit. He noted that "The church is small in very good repaire," adding, "There wants some mending of ye piews at ye bottom."

By 1874, Hazeleigh church was beginning to get a bad press. H W King, writing in his *Essexiae Ecclestiatica*, complained "It is extremely small and so utterly devoid of interest ... that I did not remain in it five minutes and took no notes ... everything is of the meanest character... there is no trace of antiquity left in the building."

The end of the 19th century saw it in a terrible condition. Since the population had moved away from the Old Hall, the church had become sorely neglected. A new, iron church was constructed in 1893 in a more convenient part of the village. Barrett's *Essex* (published in 1893) was entirely more sympathetic in his observations on the church, he states "Hazeleigh ... despite the drawbacks, as an old fashioned place of worship still remains quite in its Georgian state. Hazeleigh church is worth a visit."

Interior of Hazeleigh church, c.1930
Plan of Hazeleigh church

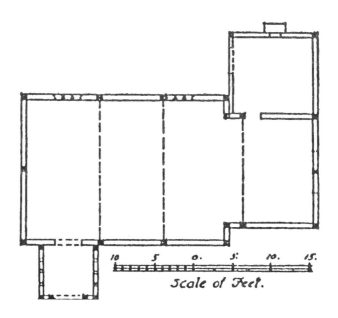

10    5    0.    5:    10.    15.

Scale of Feet.

Barrett goes on to describe a little of the inside: "The roughly whitewashed walls are rudely decorated with texts of scripture painted in the crudest of distemper colours." On the state of the structure in general he states: "From the outside one may thrust a stick through the wall of the nave into the church, so dilapidated is the entire structure."

The *Essex Review* included an article on Hazeleigh church in 1923 entitled 'Ruined and Disused Churches in Essex'. The author, Stephen Barns, states that while claims about the church's famed 'meanness' may be true, "as far as Essex is concerned it was unique, and as a specimen of cottage building for church purposes it might well have been preserved while preservation was possible." He conceded that by the 1920s the church was beyond repair and regretfully had to be pulled down.

However, he was adamant that if the church had been cared for in the 1890s it would still be standing today. He described how "The whole building had sunk some eight or nine inches from north to south with the result that the reading desk was crooked as well as the pulpit, and sounding board suspended above. Attached to the wall just above the level of the reading desk was an iron hourglass stand.

"After [1893,] neglect and decay slowly brought the building to a deplorable state of ruin. Outside the plaster had fallen away from the laths, particularly on the southern and western sides, and the porch and the timbers of the little bell turret were broken and decayed. Internally the condition was even worse, the plaster of the ceiling had fallen in, and the beams were broken away; the floor tiling displaced and broken and the whole littered with debris. The hour glass stand had disappeared, probably pilfered by some of the vandals who carved their names on the timbers and scribbled their autographs all over the plaster where it remained."

The church had at least one firm champion. A former rector, the Reverend H R Wadmore, (curate from 1848 to 1850) wrote a small book entitled *Poems by a Country Curate*. In it, he recorded his 'Recollections of Hazeleigh Church':

A little Church beside a wood
Securely sheltered from the sweeping blast;
So quiet, so secure, it seems to be
A very type of rest and all that's still.

'Tis plain and simple, here no tracer
Stretches across the windows - no fair form
Of Saint, or Martyr, or the Holy Cross
Gleams in the sunlight.

By the 1920s, the end of the church was nigh. In a local newspaper cutting entitled 'Old Hazeleigh Church - Views on its Demolition' the Reverend Brook (rector of the combined parish of Woodham Mortimer with Hazeleigh) was quoted as saying "before anything was done a public meeting was held and all present agreed that the old building should be taken down ... it should have come down a long time ago. The whole of the foundations had gone, the floor was like the waves of the sea, the roof was falling in, the ceiling was coming down and the windows were broken ... there had been no service of any kind there since 1906."

Photographs in the Essex Record Office, taken just prior to its destruction, show it to be in a sad state. After a few years acting as a mortuary chapel, it was finally demolished in 1922, Eventually the iron church was also demolished and the parish of Hazeleigh merged with that of Woodham Mortimer. There are indications that the altar rail, described by Reverend Brook as "very interesting and probably Elizabethan," was saved and given to another church. The "Beautiful Bell" of 1793 is hanging in Woodham Mortimer church. The nearby wood now covers the whole of Hazeleigh churchyard. Amongst the trees and undergrowth can still be found a number of gravestones belonging to past parishioners of Hazeleigh church.

Location: The site of the church is at the end of Hazeleigh Hall Lane, a mile south of the A414 Maldon Road. It is on private land. Contact Hazeleigh Hall or Woodham Mortimer Churchwarden before planning a visit.

Hazeleigh church.

35

Ingrave
(OS Ref: TQ 6223 9300)

The original church of St Nicholas, Ingrave, lay just south-west of Ingrave Hall, near the end of the road now known as Middle Road.

In 1710, Holman says "the church lyes in a dirty bottom near Ingrave Hall, church and chancell of one pace tiled: in a wooden frame 3 bells a shaft shingled. No monuments &c in."

An archæological excavation was undertaken by C R Crouchman in 1975. He firmly believed bricks found in the foundations were Roman.

Whether this signifies a Roman building that was adapted to become a Christian Saxon church or whether the bricks and tiles were brought from other structures around the area, is unclear. Crouchman concluded that St Nicholas was a small Norman church with an apsidal end built probably in the 12th century, perhaps like Copford or Hadleigh.

He was unsure as to whether it remained with an apsidal end until the 1734 demolition or whether it was squared off later as many others were. He also guessed that the porch was built around 1520 "under the terms of the Wallis Charity." He found both mediæval and 18th century pottery in his excavations.

Only two pictures of the church exist, both being on estate maps from 1596 and 1689. The earlier picture, by John Walker, shows the nave, chancel, a south porch and a wooden bell-frame at the west end. The second is by William Stane and I believe it to be an inaccurate sketch of the church at this time. It certainly does not appear to agree with Holman's description of the church just twenty years later.

Morant says that the "churches of West Horndon and Gingralph [Ingrave], being grown ruinous, an Act of Parliament was obtained for uniting those two parishes: and the churches being taken down, a new one of brick was built at the charge of the Rt. Hon. the late Lord Petre. It stands about the mid-way between the two ancient churches, near the mounts belonging to West Horndon Hall, whence an avenue to Burntwood [Brentwood] is made, with new plantations of trees and a basin."

Lord Petre of Thorndon Hall built the new church beside the main road (now the A128) in 1734. It is built of red brick and has a huge west tower. Pevsner described it as "the most remarkable 18th century church in the county."

From the original Ingrave church came the Tudor font and a 17th century communion table. From West Horndon came two superb brasses: one to Margaret Wake who died in 1466, and the other to Sir Richard FitzLewes and his four wives.

Today there is nothing of the structure remaining on the site. It was sited in what is now the back garden of a modern house. The exact position is difficult to pinpoint but, if access is permitted to the garden, it was to the right of the pond. There is no evidence of graves above ground although possibly these remain undisturbed below.

Location: The site is on private land. Being in the back garden of a private residence it is unlikely that the owners will take too kindly to visits from the casual passer-by. Contact the owners of Hall Farm to arrange possible access.

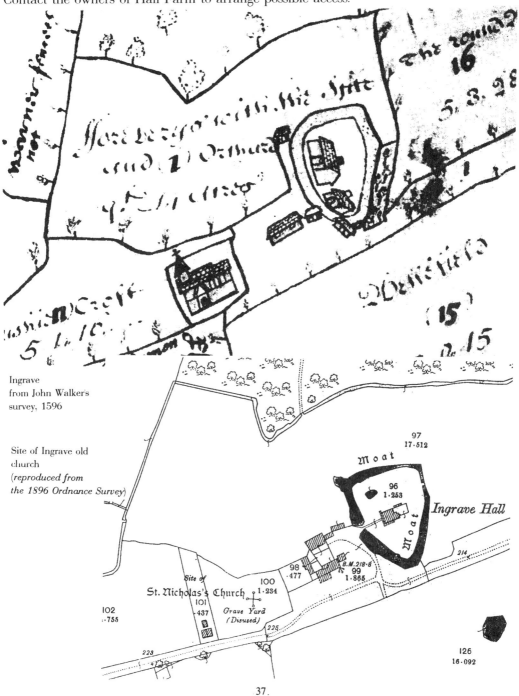

Ingrave
from John Walker's
survey, 1596

Site of Ingrave old
church
(*reproduced from
the 1896 Ordnance Survey*)

Kelvedon Hatch
(OS Ref: TL 5590 0002)

The small village of Kelvedon Hatch is about three miles from Chipping Ongar. However, the original parish church, along with Kelvedon Hall, is sited midway between the two parishes. The parish has had at least three different churches over the years.

The first parish church was mediæval. There is very little information on the substance of this old church, which is known to have been in existence from at least 1372. The second Kelvedon Hatch parish church was erected between 1740 and 1753, on the same site as its predecessor. It incorporated many floor monuments from the older building. The structure comprised a chancel and nave of red brick with a small wooden bell turret at its western end.

There were ornamental wooden pillars beside the south door. The chancel had a Venetian east window. It was restored in 1873 by subscription at a cost of £380. Some of these features are still visible today.

St Nicholas was never a grand building but served the parish well and had interesting Georgian features: quite rare in Essex churches. It is worth a visit for this reason alone. The church had many monuments and inscriptions to the Wright family, owners of the nearby Hall for almost 400 years, who finally sold the Hall in 1932.

At the end of 1893, the church and churchyard were closed to interments. A new church (also dedicated to St Nicholas) was built nearer the centre of the village. This was consecrated on 1 November, 1895. The 14th or 15th century font and the bell inscribed "Sancte Andree Ora Pro Nobis" were removed to this new church. The *Essex Review* gave a report of a number of memorials and brasses that were still in the church after its abandonment. Not all of these appear to have made the journey to the new church.

In 1945, a German rocket damaged the old church. Its current state is dismaying. The interior is inaccessible due to the collapse of the east end. A notice warns visitors that the site is dangerous. It is, however, commendable that it has not been demolished. It is at present owned by Paul Channon, lately MP for Southend West.

Location: You must first obtain permission from Kelvedon Hall to view this ruin. Notices advise visitors that the walls may be unsafe. Much of the exterior walls survive with the exception of the east wall.
Gravestones appear in lines up against the churchyard wall.

Kelvedon old church beside Kelvedon Hall

Kelvedon Hatch old church today

Langenhoe
(OS Ref: TM 0 1 38 1745)

The original church of St Andrew's, Langenhoe, was about four miles from Colchester. It is generally believed to have been a Norman structure.

Despite this, Rodwell described it as "basically mediæval in appearance."

Morant gave this description of the church in the 18th century "of one pace with the chancel, tiled: adjoining to the north wall of the Church are the ruins of an oratory, or Chapel. In a Tower of stone there is 1 Bell."

Wright adds that "in the window of the chancel of this church are many shields of arms."

In the 19th century, Reverend Parkinson was attempting to raise funds to restore the building. At 9.18 am on 22 April, 1884, his plans were thwarted when an earthquake struck. Twenty churches were reputedly damaged but Langenhoe was the worst affected. Many other buildings in the Colchester district were also wrecked. Places as far afield as Somerset, Wolverhampton and Belgium felt the effects.

Even before the earthquake, the tower was said to lean. In fact, it was likened to the tower of Pisa, and leaned due to its "age and bad foundations." The unstable tower, coupled with the fact that the church was almost at the epicentre of the shock meant that it was so badly damaged it had to be virtually demolished and rebuilt.

The Reverend W Parkinson was sitting in the rectory when the earthquake struck. He felt "a violent shock." The whole house shook for a few seconds shattering the chimneys, cracking ceilings and collapsing part of the roof. On emerging from the rectory, the Vicar beheld the sad sight of the church. "It seemed utterly ruined," he later said, "some tons of the stone battlements of the tower had been dislodged. These had fallen with great force upon the nave, which was almost entirely destroyed."

The interior suffered further still. "Roof timbers and masonry had smashed the pews and pulpit. The altar was buried under debris and the choir gallery had been ripped from its wall foundations."

The church was closed for two years, while the church was rebuilt to be re-opened in 1886. Much of the old stone and materials were used in the rebuilding. Many of the 15th century features were included in the new church - primarily the windows and doorways. The 500-year-old doors were rehung. The font and bell were kept. The octagonal font dates from the Perpendicular period showing panels with flowers in quatrefoils. The bell proclaimed "Miles Graye made me 1663." Also saved were a 17th century chair and chest.

Langenhoe was said to be one of the most haunted churches in Essex (second only to Borley). The Reverend Ernest Merryweather, rector there for twenty years, had a number of disturbing experiences, which prompted a BBC ghost hunting team to spend the night there in 1961. Nothing materialised, but ghost or no ghost, the church was again haunted with demolition.

Langenhoe church after the earthquake

The new Langenhoe church being demolished, 1962

The church was not opened again for prayers after 1959 as it was now deemed too dangerous. The last service was held on Easter Sunday of that year and the last person to be buried there was 105-year-old Mrs Joanna Locke. Ten local people volunteered to clear up the churchyard that August as it had deteriorated badly. At this stage, the church authorities were already considering Langenhoe's future and the possibility of its destruction.

Peter Wormwell of Langenhoe Hall made a spirited defence of the church in an effort to save it, writing to the *Essex County Standard* in September, 1960: "although the architects' opinion of the condition is not a good one it is my opinion that, if it is not demolished the church will still be standing when all those people standing today will have long since been buried." The authorities, however, finally decided that funds were not available for necessary repairs to make it safe and it was too dangerous to keep the church in its current state. Sadly, demolition was their conclusion.

When demolished in 1962 the church had lasted just 76 years since being rebuilt. It took just over four weeks to demolish the structure.

There are many photographs of its destruction. Its font went to North Weald church; the bell went to Abberton. The fate of the 17th century chair is not known. It was decided that the graveyard be fenced off and preserved. The parish was united with Abberton and the Parish Council maintains the graveyard. Nothing remains but a few scattered gravestones. There are no visible remains of the church with its once impressive tower. However, one can just make out the rectangular site of the ill-fated Earthquake church of Langenhoe.

Location: The site of the church is beside Langenhoe Lodge, down Langenhoe Hall Lane. This lane is east from the Colchester Road (B1025) just a mile south of Abberton. The old churchyard can be accessed through a modern white gate.

Langenhoe church, c.1905

Layer Breton
(OS Ref: TL 9495 1718)

The parish church of St Mary's was built in the Norman period and demolished in 1915. It was a simple structure comprising nave, chancel and bell turret and was approximately 46 feet by 25 feet. It derived its name from the Breton family who were Lords of the manor from Norman times until the 15th century.

By 1633 the church steeple was in disrepair and the chancel needed "boarding and glazing." In the early 1700s Holman described a grey marble gravestone situated in the chancel, with brass inscription to Alice, wife of Nicholas Breton, dated 1392. The church also had a Communion cup made in 1724. Morant says the bell turret contained a single bell.

In 1829, the newly appointed vicar, Reverend Sutton, embarked on a systematic restoration of the church, beginning with the interior. The pulpit was moved forward, the seating was altered and a children's gallery built at the east end. In 1834, a vestry was built on to the north side. Zinc troughing was erected all around the church in 1837 in an attempt to overcome the dampness. Reverend Sutton financed further extensive restoration in 1844. The bell turret was repaired and a west gallery built. to accommodate musicians. Iron beams replaced the rotting originals. The exterior and interior were painted. The church contained a tablet to Sutton, its most respected benefactor, who died on the Isle of Wight in 1855.

On 22 April, 1884, the Great Earthquake struck. There are few reports of its effect on Layer Breton church but, given the church was near its epicentre, it doubtless caused damage to the foundations. Over the next few years its condition deteriorated and eventually became unsafe. It was shored up but never properly repaired. A watercolour of the old church c.1909, painted by Thomas Simpson hangs in the replacement church.

In October, 1914, Philip Laver visited the old church and described its deplorable state in extensive detail: "The west wall of the nave, of 19th century brickwork was badly bulging and strutted up to keep it from falling; in it were two wooden square headed windows, one. above the other, the upper one having remains of a hood moulding in brick. The south wall of the nave of rubble with brick patches had one window of two lights with stone jambs and mullions, but with a flat wooden head and inserted on the east side of this window were the remains of a hood mould.

"At the angle next to the chancel was a small square buttress of two flights, having a piece of stringcourse put in upside down; this no doubt belonged to the early building. Above the buttress was a small square wooden window to light the pulpit. In the north wall of the nave the rubble was cracked throughout its height in more than one place, and contained many Roman tiles. In this wall near the chancel end was a small square headed two light window of stone.

Laver described the chancel as being of late 17th century brick. It was probably

Layer Breton old church
Layer Breton old church site today

rebuilt later when "a south square headed window made of wood, and a pointed east window, also of wood" was added.   He goes on to say "The nave walls had been plastered and the external walls are whitewashed.   Round the church at ground level were several circular openings for ventilation under the wooden floor of the pews."

The brick and timber south porch was also very dilapidated.   The 15th century south doorway was described simply as "plain." The white brick floor was also in a deplorable state at this time having been "much dug about and destroyed... [by] rabbits." The chancel arch was of the late 15th century.   "The communion table was uprooted and overthrown in quest for rabbits.   In the centre of the floor were three stone slabs, one on the south side evidently the matrix of a brass." On the north side of the church was a 19th century brick vestry.   The roofs were tiled and broken.   The wooden bell turret contained one bell.   Over the chancel arch were the Royal Arms of Victoria.

In the following year, 1915, the church was demolished. A new church of red brick with a white 'dovecote' turret was built in 1923 at a cost of £2,000.   This church contains an interesting piece of Italian sculpture of the Virgin Mary with child and a 16th century wood carving of Abraham and Isaac.   A barn opposite Layer Breton Old Rectory was used for worship until the new church was finished.

The old site is now overgrown and, apart from a few gravestones, there is little left to see.   In 1920, there remained various worked and moulded stones of the 15th century but these appear to have gone.   The most recent grave on the old site is to a former member of the household of Layer Breton Hall, opposite, buried with her husband in the 1980s.

Location: The site of the church lies opposite Layer Breton Hall at the southern end of the parish near Abberton reservoir. It lies in the middle of a copse.   The only way to gauge the site of the church is to go prepared with a photo of it, showing the relative position of the remaining tombstones.

Layer Breton.
The replacement church
on another site

Little Barling
(OS Ref: TQ 9180 8988)

Like so many other lost churches, little is known of this forgotten parish and church. If it were not for the fact that the parish of Barling Magna (Great) was still so-called, then I may have completely missed the existence of Barling Parva (Little). Even Rodwell makes no mention of its existence.

The church of that lost parish is said to have been in the vicinity of Bolt's Farm to the north of the current parish. What are thought to be the foundations of this church were dug up in a field there just a few years ago. In dry summer months, it is said to be still possible to make out the faint outline of the church from the air.

This scant information is all I have been able to glean. There is no mention of it in the Essex Record Office and therefore no description of its structure, exact location or reason for its demise.

Location: Said to be near Bolt's Farm in the parish of Barling. Apply to the farmer before entering the land as it is private property.

Etching of Little Birch Hall and church from Mullman's *History of Essex*, 1771 (*reproduced with the permission of Essex Record Office*)

*Little Birch Hall, the Seat of James Round Esq.*

Little Birch
(OS Ref: TL 9501 2078)

The ruined church of St Mary's, Little Birch, sits among undergrowth, off the beaten track, near the site of the former Birch Hall. It is an impressive ruin: perhaps the best in Essex. It is probably my favourite 'lost church'. I was therefore delighted to hear talk of clearing away the nettles and brambles and opening it to the public (However, this has not yet happened). According to the current sign, "trespassers" are threatened with prosecution.

The church fell into disuse in 1598. Morant wrote in 1768 that the roof was gone and the church ruinous. This is probably why no gravestones remain. There were at one time, monuments to the Eldred family but these followed the surviving family to Earls Colne. This church then fell into ruin.

Arthur Mee described it in 1940 thus: "The big chancel is 600 years old and so is the broken tower, though its upper brickwork is Tudor. The nave was built by the Normans who... made good use of the Roman bricks so plentiful round Colchester. Here they are, in the pilasters, at the corners of the walls, and in the doorway."

The chancel is 26½ feet by 16 feet and includes 14th century windows and doorway. The chancel arch of about 1400 has largely disappeared. The nave is 31½ feet by 19 feet and has 12th and 14th century windows. Traces of the rood stairs have all but disappeared. The south doorway is largely destroyed.

Considering St Mary's has been neglected for 400 years, it was in remarkably good condition on my first visit in May, 1995. The walls appeared quite sturdy. They are mainly stone with many red tiles and bricks taken from nearby Roman ruins. These materials possibly came from a local Roman villa.

The interior is quite ruinous. Dead leaves and nettles cover the floor of the chancel and nave but there is still much detail left. Some of the old features can be discerned, such as the remains of the piscina in the east of the south wall, by the chancel window. The east window is entirely dilapidated; indeed one can walk right through the site of the east wall. The only part of the chancel arch to remain is a small fragment on the north side and the remains of the pillar on the south side.

However, most of the arches to the remaining windows have survived.

The tower is in good condition. The bottom section is from the 14th century; the top and the stair turret were built in the Tudor-period in red brick. It is 6½ feet square and contains a nice 14th century west window. Much of its tracery survives. The interior of the tower still retains some of the original wood that held the bell.

There remains some old graffiti round the tower walls. None of the windows in the church retain their glazing and the roof is missing. No monuments are visible inside the church; no graves are in evidence outside. For all that, St Mary's still makes an excellent shrine and well worth the visit. A word of warning: at certain times of the year, you may come across a pheasant or two in the churchyard!

Location: This ruin is not easy to find. Taking the B1022, there is a road to the left just before Fountain Lane. Follow the lane towards Layer de la Haye. Opposite a small copse called 'Sybils' is a small lane which will warn you against trespassing. The church is on the right, next to the site of Birch Hall. The ruin is on private land. I suggest you contact Mr Round of Great Birch before venturing on to it.

Little Birch church ruins today
The tower, Little Birch church

Little Henny
(OS Ref: TL 8676 3779)

The remains of this small church stand in the grounds of The Ryes Boarding School, a few yards south-east of the building. The site lies about half a mile north-west of the parish church of Great Henny. I visited the site on a cold, foggy January morning in 1996. An eight-year-old pupil showed me around the ruins.

This tiny ancient building was ruinous by the time of Holman. As he described it in about 1710: "everything of the church have been prostrated... only about two yards of stone wall to be seen standing."

In the time of Morant, the parish was still distinct from that of Great Henny. Warwick Rodwell believes that it was "A simple rectangular building, Norman with alterations. Long since demolished; foundations excavated and the walls rebuilt up to a height of approx. 30 inches." It was by then part of a landscaped garden.

In 1930, Fairweather describes "the scanty remains of this little church" as being "of interest to the ecclesiological student as those of a building finally destroyed some three hundred years ago." He tells us of two periods of construction. The first building was perhaps constructed at the end of the 12th century of Barnack stone. This was a rectangular building 46 feet 4 inches by 15 feet 7 inches. All the walls were 3 feet 6 inches thick except the west wall which was thinner at 2 feet 9 inches and held firm by buttresses.

The only door was in the south wall (at the western end). It is thought that the building's demise began when the east end collapsed, having been built injudiciously on soft ground.

The church was reconstructed in the 14th or 15th century. The replacement building was 37 feet 2 inches by 15 feet 7 inches. The problematic eastern end was cut off and a new wall was erected. The remainder was rebuilt on the existing bases, round parts of the former building. The south wall in particular had suffered from subsidence. At some point, buttresses were added to shore up this and the north wall. Part of a small stone stoup also survives.

The destruction of Little Henny church occurred at the end of the 16th or early 17th century. Fairweather concludes, "the final end of the building was unquestionably by fire, as the entire floor level was covered by a layer of charcoal." There are few surviving monuments. On my visit, one was perched on top of the north wall. It bore the remains of a broken cross. The foundations are 3 feet 6 inches high in places. Fairweather's excavations uncovered both mediæval pottery, fragments of mediæval glass and some Roman dressed green marble. My diminutive guide told me that the graves had been moved down to the roadside. No evidence of them remains today.

Location: The Ryes School lies down a small lane, south-east from the A131 from Bulmer Tye. Permission should be sought from the staff before visiting the ruins, which lie a few yards from the school.

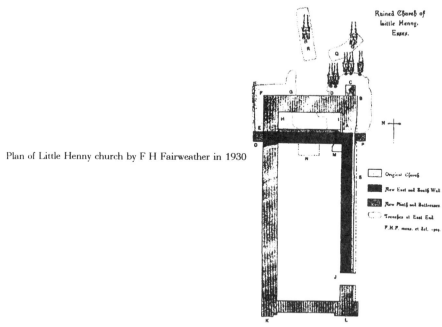

Plan of Little Henny church by F H Fairweather in 1930

The remains of Little Henny today

Little Holland
(OS Ref: TM 2090 1667)

Little Holland is about two miles from Clacton town centre, on a corner of the road leading to Great Holland. The church site is about 60 yards south-east of Little Holland Hall. Originally a mile from the sea, the ruins are now only about 200 yards from the cliff. Its dedication is unknown and no parish registers exist. The parish of Little Holland always had a very small population.

Trial excavations by Kenneth Walker in 1960 revealed a simple rectangular Norman building approximately 65 feet by 22 feet. Walker noted that the nave is 'almost identical' in size to that of Little Clacton, just three miles away. It is thought that they may have been built by the same builder, to the same design. It has been suggested that it was built in the first half of the 12th century. The building consisted of a chancel, a nave, a south porch and a steeple.

David Andrews and Howard Brooks wrote about this lost church for the publication *Essex Archæology and History* in 1989. They divided the church's construction into four distinct stages. The first was a single-celled church with an apsidal end, built in the 11th or 12th century. This was built of 'unmortared septaria block laid in clay'. It was 44 feet by 19½ feet at this time.

The second stage occurred in the late 12th or 13th century. The nave was lengthened by 12 feet at the west end and the apsidal end was squared off. The extension of the nave is thought to have accommodated the belfry. The church was now approximately 56 feet 5 inches by 19 feet 5 inches at its widest point. The walls were over 4 feet thick. None of the original was demolished - the new was simply added to the existing structure.

The third phase consisted of mediæval rebuilding in the 13th and 14th centuries, including the east and west walls. This was with mortared septaria and flint. The fourth period of reconstruction took place from the 15th century to the mid-17th century. This included the use of red bricks in the refreshing and building of the buttresses.

The church is generally thought to have suffered decay due to its "exposed situation towards the sea, [it] was beat down by the frequent recurrence of storms." Severe storms caused erosion down much of the Essex coast during 1376 and 1377. By 1428, Little Holland itself was suffering from the ravages of the sea. In the same, year, Little Holland was declared exempt from taxation due to there being less than ten inhabitants. In the 1640s, it was reported that the east coast was losing land daily to the sea. Andrews and Brooks cited the coastal erosion as the principal reason for what seems to have been economic decline at Little Holland.

A visitation by church authorities in 1633 reported that "Their chauncell wants pavinge and glazinge and the walls thereof want pargetting round about and whitinge with inside." The church was obviously in a poor state of repair, though still standing.

A Parochial Inquisition of 1650 found there to be fewer than 60 families in the parish - all near Great Clacton. It was decided that the parish should be united with Great Clacton, and so it has remained to this day. The visitation of 1683 recorded that the church had been demolished about 24 years and its bells were in the yard of the Hall. It is estimated that it was demolished around 1656-1659.

A faculty was granted in 1696 to move the church's bells to Great Clacton. It declared the church had been "for at least these forty years demolished and the place almost eaten up by the seas, so that it is almost impossible to rebuild the same: And that the inhabitants of Little Holland do now repair to Much Clackton... to hear divine services and enjoy all the other privileges and conveniences of the said church."

On demolition, locals helped themselves to the ancient stone; such that the ruins were soon taken down to ground level. In 1977, Warwick Rodwell mourned the fact that the site was, "now so disturbed that it may be regarded as archæologically destroyed.' However, in 1987 Anglia Secure Homes built sheltered housing near the site and the Archæological Section of the Essex County Council carried out an excavation of the foundations of the church, thereby preventing damage to them when building work commenced. The site retains features for the local historian or interested observer to discover, since its outline is still clearly visible. The ruins, up to a foot high, are now covered in grass.

Location: The ruins are set beside Little Holland Hall at the above Ordnance Survey map reference, on the corner of the road from Clacton to Great Holland (the B1032). A small stone tablet announces "Ancient Burial Site" on the path outside the ruins.

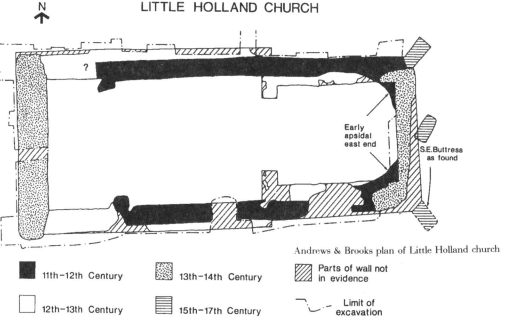

N ↑          LITTLE HOLLAND CHURCH

Early apsidal east end

S.E. Buttress as found

?

Andrews & Brooks plan of Little Holland church

- ■ 11th–12th Century
- □ 12th–13th Century
- ▨ 13th–14th Century
- ▤ 15th–17th Century
- ▧ Parts of wall not in evidence
- Limit of excavation

Little Stambridge
(OS Ref: TO 8874 9195)

A number of sources name this church All Saints, while others describe it as St Mary's. Whichever the correct dedication, it was a small church consisting of just a chancel, a nave with a small wooden belfry and a south porch. It was sited next to Little Stambridge Hall, barely a mile from Great Stambridge. Originally a mediæval church, it was greatly restored in the mid-1800s. Wright described the pre-restored structure as "a small ancient building; the nave and church of one pace; the arms of Bohun appear in the window of the belfry." In 1870, it underwent complete restoration, at a cost of £280. This was a vain but valiant attempt by the Hall's occupier, Mr Keys, to keep the church open.

A little after this H W King described it as "barbarously rebuilt of red brick upon the old foundations." It appears to have contained little of the original structure at this stage. King maintained that just the south doorway and perhaps the interior structure of the belfry was retained from the original. The wooden spire was, as usual, at the west end but had been modernised with 19th century weatherboards.

The bell tower housed just one bell. But this lone bell was something of a rarity. It was made by Richard Bowler of Colchester, master of the famous bell-maker Miles Graye the elder. The window frames were unusual, being simply made of wood. The Arms of the de Bohun family appeared in the belfry window.

However, King was not at all impressed with Little Stambridge church, describing it as "a paltry edifice in its present condition." The font was of the Perpendicular period. It was the only feature of the church that found favour with King who described it as "of good proportion and neat design, octangular with concave sides." This design was so similar to that of Great Stambridge that King speculated as to whether the same man designed the two.

In 1880, due to the sparseness of the population, the two parishes of Great and Little Stambridge were united. This spelt the end of one of the churches. There was little doubt as to which would eventually close. The church at Little Stambridge saw its final marriage in 1886 and its last baptism in 1887.

At a vestry meeting on 27 December, 1887, "it was decided that in consequence of the dilapidated condition of the building and there being no monument or mural tablets and no architectural feature worth preserving in the same.... The removal of the building it being no longer required for services in consequence of the union of the parishes of Great and Little Stambridge."

The church was finally demolished in 1891. Much of the fabric of the old church, including the ancient piscina" went to St Mark's church in Southend. The *East Anglian Magazine* commented "One hardly knows why such relics should be removed from their original surroundings or what relation they can bear to the brand new fabric besides which they clearly must appear out of keeping."

Nowadays a copse of trees stands in front of Little Stambridge Hall. Gravestones can be seen scattered within this copse. The old church was, no doubt, sited in the large rectangle where no graves stand. There is little of the fabric left, save a few scattered pieces of stone and red tile. The entrance to the churchyard can easily be discerned on the south side.

Location: Take the Stambridge road from Rochford, east towards Great Stambridge. Little Stambridge Hall Road is about half a mile before Great Stambridge church. The church was situated near the end of the lane, in front of the Hall.

Little Stambridge church, c.1880 (*reproduced with the permission of Essex Record Office*)

Little Stambridge churchyard today

Little Wenden
(OS Ref: TL 5080 3620)

Once there were three Wendens: Wenden Lofts, Great Wenden and Little Wenden. The parish church of Little Wenden was situated "on the left side of the road from Wenden Lofts to Great Wenden." Its dedication is unknown. The only reference I have been able to find describing its appearance is in an old will which mentions the church as having a tower.

The churches of Little Wenden and Great Wenden were less than a mile apart and the joint population was not large enough to keep up payments for both churches. Therefore, at the request of the parishioners, and with the consent of the Earl of Suffolk (patron of both churches), the parishes of Great and Little Wenden were united in 1662 by Bishop Sheldon. Great Wenden then became known as Wendens Ambo.

Little Wenden's church and Great Wenden's vicarage, both being ruinous, were pulled down. Rates were assessed with two parts to Great Wenden and one part to Little Wenden. Little Wenden's parsonage was repaired and appropriated to the Vicar of Wendens Ambo.

Warwick Rodwell observed "The site of little Wenden church is recorded by the Ordnance Survey as lying under plough-land, adjacent to the rectory. It is, however, probably in the rectory garden." The present owners of the 'Old Vicarage' have their own theory. They believe that when the vicarage was rebuilt it was moved to the site of the old church, making use of its foundations. The peaceful spirit of the present building confirms this theory for them.

When the M11 was built (on the approximate site of the Second Edition OS map church site) evidence of Little Wenden church was first sought, but none was found. On searching the area for tiles and stone very little has been found - just a small amount of (possibly dressed) stone and large flints which possibly came from the church. The rest may have been plundered by local residents for buildings, walls, or repairing Wendens Ambo church.

There may be one other part of the church that survives. It is believed that the timbers in the roof of the Old Vicarage are much older than the building itself and so must have been taken from an existing building. This building was possibly Little Wenden church.

Location: The site of Little Wenden church is open to debate. It was possibly under ploughed land to the west as mapped on the Second Edition OS Map (1897), beneath the concrete of the M11 motorway, in the garden of the Old Vicarage (as stated by Rodwell) or even under that very building! In the absence of further clues, its exact position remains uncertain.

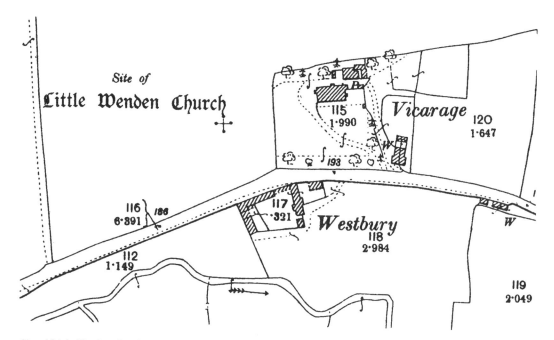

Site of Little Wenden church as shown on the 1897 Ordnance Survey

Pieces of dressed stone found in the vicarage garden

Loughton
(OS Ref: TQ 4389 9645)

The original church of the parish of Loughton was dedicated to St Nicholas. It was situated on what is now Rectory Road, beside Loughton Hall. The earliest mention of a church was in a charter granted to Loughton in 1177 by Henry II, but the church may have stood for many years previously.

St Nicholas consisted of a nave, chancel, north aisle, south porch and a weather-boarded tower with shingled spire. The nave and chancel were both about 18 feet wide. They were about 56 feet in combined length.

There was a large 15th century window at the east end of the chancel. In the chancel's south wall there was a two-light window and a low-side window. The north aisle measured about 18 feet by 54 feet. A chapel was situated at its east end, divided from the rest of the aisle by a wooden screen. The tower was built in two stages - stone at the base with a dark wooden belfry.

It is believed that St Nicholas had three bells. One of these was apparently sold at the end of the 18th century. The remaining two were recast to become the fifth bell of St John's. In 1737, the tower and spire were repaired and general repairs were made in 1825-7 and 1829.

In 1836, Loughton Hall was demolished. The church had already become isolated and it was now even more removed from the village centre. A new church, dedicated to St John, was therefore built in 1846 in a more convenient location in Blind Lane. Built in Norman style in yellow brick it consists of a nave, central tower, chancel transepts and a north porch.

It was decided to demolish St Nicholas, in the hope that some of the proceeds would offset the building of St John's. However, it only raised £89, instead of the expected £250. The chancel remained, to be turned into a mortuary chapel. Within thirty years, with the huge expansion of Loughton, it was decided to build another church on the site of the old. In 1877, what was left of the old church was demolished and a replacement St Nicholas was built a few yards to the west, in a similar style to the old. For many years, this church was used privately by the residents of the new Loughton Hall, which had just been built.

It is believed that the original plate was destroyed when the former Loughton Hall burnt down. There are several 16th and 17th century brasses in the replacement St Nicholas. There is a late-16th century painting of the Annunciation and early-16th century glass in the north and south windows: all thought to have come from the original church.

The gable of the porch is reported to include carved bargeboards from the old church.

Location: The site of the old church is just yards from the east window of its replacement. The outline of its structure is still visible, as are many of its monuments. Apply to the warden for the key of the new St Nicholas to view the original glass and brasses, since access is restricted to services. The site of the old church is however accessible at all times.

St Nicholas, Loughton, 1600
The site of St Nicholas, Loughton, old church, metres east of the new church

Manningtree
(OS Ref: TM 1076 3185)

The church of St Michael and All Angels was in Manningtree High Street, replacing a much more ancient chapel in a less convenient position. Some of the stone from the earlier monument is believed to have been incorporated into the replacement building. The earlier chapel had suffered much at the hands of the Reformation and fell into disuse. The inhabitants of Manningtree feared their town would be open to invasion by pirates or other seafaring opportunists while they were worshipping at Mistley. So, in 1616 they chose a more convenient site for the replacement church: the High Street. The frontage of the north aisle formed an integral part of the High Street until its demolition in 1967. The churchyard was at the rear.

The first construction consisted simply of a nave and two aisles. It was built in brick, septaria and flint and featured an interesting 17th century hammerbeam roof. Some of the church timbers are reputed to have been reused wood from old ships.

The nave was 50 feet by 15 feet 5 inches. Galleries over the two aisles were erected in about 1788. The south aisle was rebuilt in 1821. A chancel was finally added in 1839. It had a small bell-tower and contained a 15th century octagonal font.

St Michael and All Angels' was elevated to the status of a parish church in 1840, having previously been a chapel to its mother church in Mistley. The church could hold an impressive congregation of 1,250 during this period.

The building also housed an interesting collection of artifacts. There was a memorial to Thomas Ormond, erected in 1748. The 'cloth worker' was burned to death during the reign of Queen Mary I in 1555, for his religious convictions. There was a collection of plate cup, cover and two patens. The Bishop of London, William Laud, later Archbishop to Charles I, gave all these to the church in 1633. There was also a fine painting by John Constable which Scarfe says is "now safely at Feering", but has recently been sold at auction.

In 1899, it was not considered cost effective to carry out a substantial reconstruction of St Michael and All Angels, so the congregation made the best of the existing structure. At some time around then, the church was closed. In December, 1901, it was reopened and renovated. New pine seats replaced the old-fashioned high pews. A new floor was laid. A new pulpit, lectern, chancel rail and choir stalls were fitted, at a total cost of £700.

The church remained in use until 1964. Between 1957 and 1964 a number of examinations were carried out in order to save the timbers of the nave roof. During repair work it was found that these massive hidden oak timbers were so decayed by rot and beetle that the nave was in danger of collapsing. The estimated cost of restoration was £22,500: the same cost of a replacement, which could be situated more conveniently in the centre of the village.

A 'Dangerous Structure' notice was posted by Tendring District Council in December, 1966, and insurance cover was withdrawn. Part of the church was demolished. The only part left was the High Street wall of the nave, the chancel and the vestry. Despite much vehement protestation against demolition, no funds were forthcoming and it was decided to amalgamate the two parishes of Mistley and Manningtree. Demolition was completed in December, 1967.

The sealed vault under the site was still in existence when the church was demolished. This contained coffins to the Alston family, old brewers in Manningtree. A small number of houses, erected in the early 1970s, stand on the former site of the church. The only surviving relic is a section of the western-most buttress and a small part of that wall.

Location: The church stood in the middle of Manningtree High Street. A plaque indicates the site. All that can be seen today is a section of the west wall and a single buttress.

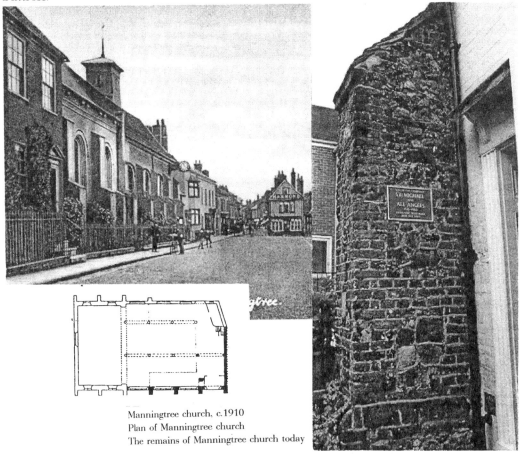

Manningtree church, c.1910
Plan of Manningtree church
The remains of Manningtree church today

Markshall
(OS Ref: TL 8409 3525)

The parish of Markshall lies two miles north of Great Coggeshall. Morant tells us that the original church of St Michael; "stands near the mansion house, and consists of a body of the same pace with the chancel. At the west end there is a wooden turret, containing 1 bell." The 'mansion house', Marks Hall, was a Tudor structure surrounded by a wooded deer park. The nearby mediæval church comprised a nave, chancel and bell-turret. During the 17th century, the west window held a portrait of an armed knight bearing the Arms of Markshall on his surcoat.

By 1875 St Michael's had changed dramatically. The mediæval church was demolished by General Philip Honywood and a new octagonal brick building, this time dedicated to St Margaret was erected.

Mrs Frances Honywood then added a tower and carried out extensive renovations - some sources say she had it virtually rebuilt. A new altarpiece, a fine painting representing the taking down of Jesus from the cross, was now in residence.

A number of memorials to the Honywood family could also be seen in the church. There was a tablet to an earlier Mrs Honywood - Mary, who died in 1620, aged 93. She left behind 16 children, 144 grandchildren, 228 great-grandchildren and 9 great-great-grandchildren: a total of 397 descendants. This memorial now resides in Great Coggeshall church.

Several other memorials to members of the Honywood family were taken to Colchester and can be seen in the garden beside the Holly Trees Museum. They include one of Sir Thomas, who took a leading part in the siege of Colchester and was brother-in-law to Sir Harry Vane.

Many others were bricked up in the vaults. In the mid-19th century the church was extensively altered and extended. This work included an enlarged chancel and nave.

By the 1920s, the local parishioners were frequenting Coggeshall church instead. Markshall church therefore became redundant. It was finally demolished in 1932. The oak choir-stalls, the reading desk and the brass lectern were brought to Coggeshall. The clock mechanism from the church is now displayed in the Visitor's Centre. An old bell made by Richard Bowler, dated 1595, was housed within the church but the fate of this ancient relic is not know to me. At least one publication states that this bell is housed in the Visitor's Centre. However, it is not there and what is more, the curator at the Visitor's Centre has never seen it!

The plate included a cup and cover-paten of 1628. The fate of these is uncertain; they were probably sent to Coggeshall church. The Parishes of Markshall and Coggeshall were then amalgamated. The parish registers, surviving from 1582, are housed at the Essex Record Office. A few tombstones dating from the early 19th century to the 1920s are still in existence, in the well-tended churchyard. A new altar has been built and the rector of Coggeshall holds services at the site a couple of times a year. The three-storey Hall (mostly rebuilt in 1609) was demolished in 1951.

Location: The site of the church is on Marks Hall Estate off Marks Hall Road, a little north-west of Coggeshall. "The Thomas Phillips Price Trust" now maintains the site. The estate provides a beautiful walk on a fine day with lakes, a walled garden and huge tracts of parkland.

Marks Hall Church

Marks Hall, mansion and church.

Site of Marks Hall church today

Mashbury
(OS Ref. TL 6519 1188)

The small parish of Mashbury lies six miles north-west of Chelmsford. Now united with the Chignals (St James, Smealy and St Mary) the church sits isolated, opposite Mashbury Hall. Morant and Wright had little to say of the church other than that it was plain, of one pace, tiled and with a steeple containing three bells.

It is a small church of Norman origin with no known dedication. The walls are a mixture of flint, rubble and Roman bricks. The chancel is 23 feet by 19 feet and mainly mid-12th century in date. It may have once had an apsidal west end. The nave is 35 feet by 21 feet and has two small Norman windows; one in the north and one in the south walls. The nave also contains two 14th century windows. According to Worley, since the windows and doorways of the nave are so narrow, this suggests that "the builders had an eye for defence."

The north doorway is quite plain but contains some attractive 13th century ironwork. The south has elaborate 12th century decoration with, as Worley puts it, "chevron mouldings of the arch, the carved capitals on which it rests and the star-like ornament of the tympanum."

In the 15th century this small church was extensively altered. The chancel arch was rebuilt and chancel extended eastward. It is possible that at this time the more usual square end replaced an apsidal end. The Tudor red brick porch was built about 1500. The roofs of both the nave and the porch are from the 15th century.

The 17th century octagonal oak pulpit is not present at the church. I have been unable to determine its whereabouts. Perhaps it has found a new home in a nearby church. Neither can I locate the 15th century chest; described as being "strong with bands of iron and seven hinges." This was still in the church earlier in this century.

Fragments of old glass - a 14th century piece showing the figure of a saint and a 16th century piece showing faces of leopards - still appear in the windows. There were a number of watercolours by William Hole over the altar including one of the Nativity. These are no longer apparent in the building.

In about 1865 (some sources say 1872) the church was struck by lightning. The subsequent fire destroyed the bell-turret, roof and melted the two bells. The bell turret was rebuilt in 1892 and recently (1982) described by Hough as "a pretty little nineteenth century bell turret." The 15th century (or 17th century as Hewett describes it) wooden framework supporting the old turret, survived the fire.

The church appears to have been in good repair during 1920s when the RCHM reported on it. None of the other 20th century sources I have researched mention its neglect so presumably this happened in the past twenty years or so. Today, the structure appears to be quite sound but the interior needs clearing. It is, however, well worth a visit for its pleasant location.

Mashbury interior, 1999

Location: Mashbury church is halfway between the Chignals and the Easters. Take the road between Chignal Smealy and Good Easter. The sign for Mashbury Hall will point you down a line. The church stands opposite the Hall. Please seek permission to view the church as it is on private land. If you obtain the key and have problems unlocking the door - try the key upside down!

Superb Norman south doorway at Mashbury

65

Mayland
(OS Ref: TL 9242 0052)

Mayland's old church, dedicated to St Barnabas, was on a hill two miles west of Southminster. The only description I have found of the original structure is by Morant and is a little sketchy, "The church is tiled and so is the chancel. In a wooden frame, boarded with a spire shingled, are three bells." Wright describes the original church as being "a small building, pleasantly situated on an eminence ... belonged with the manor to the abbey of St Osyth..."

It was reported to the Bishop of Rochester by a humble petition of the Vicar and Churchwardens that: "the ancient parochial church ... of Mayland... is in a very dilapidated state and does not afford sufficient accommodation for the parishioners and inhabitants of the same parish who are desirous of attending the public worship of Almighty God"

Therefore a new church was required which would be "large, more commodious and substantial" and in "a more convenient site in the said parish." The new church was built in 1867, about 300 yards north of the old. It was designed by Philip Hardwick (the younger) and built of Kentish Ragstone in the Early English style. It too, was consecrated to Saint Barnabas.

The new church consists of a chancel, nave and south porch with a bellcote at the west end. The old bell, made by Miles Graye in 1662, is housed in an open gable at the east end of the nave. The old church's plate was transferred to the new church. This comprised a paten of 1568 and a cup from approximately the same date. The Parish Registers, dating from 1748, were also brought to the new church.

When the old church was demolished around 1873, the materials were salvaged and sold. The proceeds were used to repair the old churchyard fence. It was decided that when pulling down the church: "it will not be necessary to interfere with any old graves... it is intended to leave the flat tombstones on the floor now inside the said old church and to level the earth with the ground outside." It was further required that the "monuments or tablets" from the old church be "carefully preserved" in the new.

The remains of the original church of St Barnabas lie in the back garden of a cottage. A memorial cross tells of the its passing.

Gravestones are grouped to show the approximate site. Among them are a couple of attractive gravestones from the 18th century.

Location: Approaching the brow of Mayland Hill from the north, the gravestones can just about be discerned from the road. For a closer inspection, first gain permission from the owner of the cottage garden that encompasses the site.

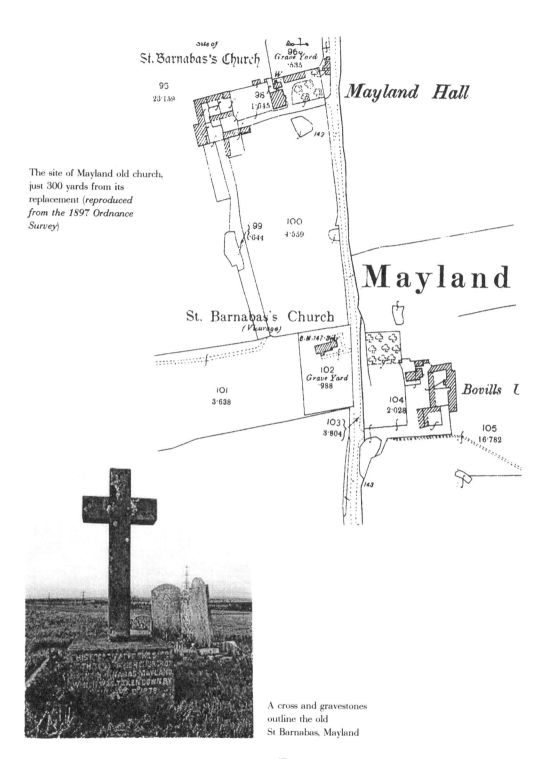

The site of Mayland old church, just 300 yards from its replacement (*reproduced from the 1897 Ordnance Survey*)

A cross and gravestones outline the old St Barnabas, Mayland

Mile End, Colchester
(OS Ref: TL 9928 2675)

The old church of St Michael stood about half a mile south from the present church, beside the Rectory. It was on the east side of the main road, a mile from Colchester town. A stone stood beside the road declaring this fact and is thought to be the reason why the parish became known as 'Mile End'. St Michael's was originally part of the parish of St Peter's but became separate by 1254. It would therefore appear that the old church predates this time.

Mile End church was in need of regular repair from 1582 onwards.

In about 1700 the eastern part of the chancel was in a ruinous condition. At this point the chancel was demolished and replaced. Possibly, the wooden western bell turret and a western gallery were added at this time. According to Morant, it was "...at one pace with the chancel, and very small: At the west end, there is a little wooden turret, containing one Bell."

In 1825, the historian, Thomas Cromwell, commented that "The church, dedicated to St Michael, is agreeably situated, but small, and of mean appearance." Just a few years later, Wright echoes this when he says "The church dedicated to St Michael is very small; it has a nave and chancel, with a wooden turret at the west end.' The handsome mansion inhabited by the rector is beside the churchyard, and commands a fine view of Colchester."

The church was demolished in about 1854 when a new church was erected in a more populated place. The site of the old church and graveyard is now in Rectory Close. Here, mediæval rubble foundations of the nave still remain near the Rectory of 1842. It was approximately 18 feet wide, but its length is more difficult to gauge as there are no remains of the chancel. Two pieces of moulded stonework are visible near the churchyard entrance.

The replacement church designed by Edward Charles Hakewill - which was also dedicated to St Michael - was built in 1854 in the Early English style. In 1887, a clock was installed to celebrate Queen Victoria's Golden Jubilee.

Ten years later, two extra bells were added to the church, in celebration of her Diamond Jubilee.

Location: The site of the old church lies down Rectory Road, about a mile north of Colchester Town Centre. The outline of the nave is still discernible. Also, several gravestones survive - though not in situ.

St Michael's, Mile End

The remains of St Michael's today

Mistley Heath
(OS Ref: TM 1287 3101)

Mistley has had three churches. The site of the mediæval building at Mistley Heath, dedicated to St Mary, lies about a mile south-east of the present church. The walls were of flint and septaria-rubble, with dressings of limestone. It consisted of a nave, chancel, south aisle, west tower and south porch.

In about 1710, Holman described Mistley church as being: "pleasantly seated on the top [of] an hill on rising ground not far from the channel ... a delightful prospect far and near. The church has a south aisle leaded the chancel of one pace tyled a tower of stone 5 bells. This church was newly built but the want of due course the body of the church fell in with the south isle only the tower and chancel standing."

The south porch was built around 1500 and survived the rest of the church by about 250 years. The Rigby family used it as a private chapel for many years. In the 1930s, Mee described it as having: "a moulded plinth inlaid with panels of flint and the buttresses and the doorway have much beauty in them." Scarfe explained that the plinth was "given c.1520 by Richard Damell, whose mark survives prominently in the spandrels." The porch survived until 1972 when it was finally bulldozed.

All that can be see today is the outline of the building: a few feet of wall and the sunken rectangle of the ruins. These are a foot or so high in parts. Graves are still dotted around the old churchyard.

Location: Mistley Heath church is on the bend of the road opposite the old rectory. It lies on private land so permission must besought before visiting. Sheep now graze where once a flock of another type congregated.

Mistley Thorn/Towers
OS Ref: TM 1165 3195)

As the years passed the population of Mistley drifted away from Mistley Heath and closer to the river Stour. Mistley Heath church therefore started to decline early in the 18th century. It finally became redundant in 1735 when a brick built church at Mistley Thorn replaced it. This was a plain building of no particular note until it was drastically altered by the designs of Robert Adam.

The building was consecrated by the Bishop of London on 6 June, 1735, and soon underwent much alteration. In 1776 it was extravagantly enlarged by Robert Adam - this included adding two massive twin towers - one at each end. The best description I have read is by Scarfe "this was given Tuscan porticoes on the north, and south sides, and twin square towers, supported by free standing Tuscan columns and surmounted by cupolas with Ionic colonnades; one serving as west tower, the other still containing the reredos (with Ten Commandments), an azure ceiling with gilt emblem of the

Trinity, and the plans of Robert Adam engraved by John Roberts." An early print shows it in this finished state.

This new church, however, did not serve the community of Mistley for very long. In 1866, only 90 years after Adam's impressive rebuild, a report decided that the church was beyond repair as it was riddled with dry rot. In 1870, it was demolished. The east and west towers were retained as navigation points. In 1871, a new St Mary's was built of Kentish ragstone in the 14th century style. Its tower and spire are an impressive 140 feet high.

Location: Mistley Towers is on the main Manningtree to Harwich road. They can be visited most days and the keys are available locally.

Plan of Mistley Towers church
Mistley Towers church, c.1870

Base of the tower
of Mistley Heath church

71

Morrell Roding
(OS Ref: TL 5650 1531)

The dedication of Morrell Roding church is unknown. Both Morant and Wright describe "the little church, or chapel, near Cames Hall [sic]" as being "of timber and mortar ... sometime ago to be seen converted into a pigeon house" before being demolished. No further description of its appearance has come to light.

Morrell Roding church stood inside the moat surrounding Cammass Hall, which lies just a couple of miles south-east of Hatfield Broad Oak church. The structure is said to have stood in the north-west corner of the garden. One side of the moat still exists, so the position can be judged from this. Earlier editions of the Ordnance Survey map show its approximate location.

Morrell Roding took its name from a former owner of Cammass Hall. According to Wright, Morrell Roding was "formerly a parish but has become a hamlet to White Roding, yet the suit and service of the court leet, by ancient custom, belongs to the hundred of Harlow."

Nowadays the two parishes are combined, Morrell Roding disappeared from our maps about 150 years ago making the parish name Morrell Roding obsolete. The ancient parish dates back to before 1320 but even at this early date, it was considered part of the parish of White Roding.

During this time, Morrell Roding was considered as a hamlet rather than a village in its own right. It appears to have had a chapel rather than a parish church. The acreage of Morrell Roding was little more than one square mile, probably encompassing Walker's Farm, Prows Farm, Philpotts and Cammass Hall. It is believed that, at no time during its history, did the parish contain more than 40 people!

Location: The site of Morrell Roding church is within the grounds of Cammass Hall. This is a private residence so please contact the owners for permission to view the site.

Cammass Hall

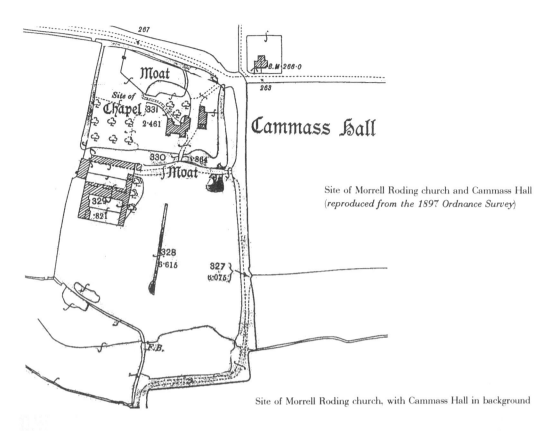

Cammass Hall

Site of Morrell Roding church and Cammass Hall
(*reproduced from the 1897 Ordnance Survey*)

Site of Morrell Roding church, with Cammass Hall in background

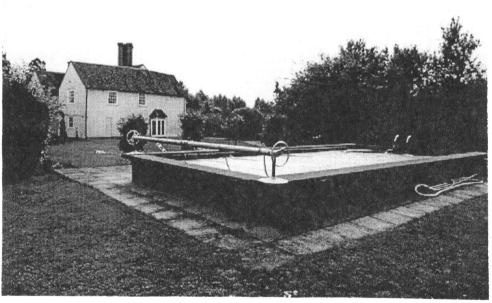

Mose (or Moze)
(OS Ref: TM 1995 2590)

St Mary's church at Mose (Anglo-Saxon for 'marsh') was south-east of Mose Hall. As early as the late 17th century it was entirely ruinous. No description of the church prior to its ruin seems to exist. Symonds found a few of the windows worthy of note but leaves us with no other impression of its structure. In the early 18th century, Holman said of it: "Some ruins appear covered with briars and thorns: not enclosed but lies open."

By the 1670s, the church had become dilapidated. The two churches of Mose and Beaumont were quite close and both parishes had the same incumbent. Impoverished parishioners could no longer afford to keep up the living of both churches. In 1678, the eleven farmers of Mose decided they could no longer finance the repair of their church. Morant states: "their parish church become very ruinous, and ready to fall down, the steeple thereof being already fallen... the patron and Rector enabled to pull down the church of Mose, and to employ the materials towards the repairs of the church of Beaumont."

The parish was therefore united with,that of Beaumont by Act of Parliament. The stone and timber from the derelict church was carried to St Leonard's, Beaumont, to help to repair the fabric of that church. It was decided that the ground where the church stood should be fenced off and the churchyard should continue to be used for burials and 'for no other use.' Morant added: "All tithes and other duties, heretofore due payable to the incumbent of the church of Mose, shall hereafter be paid, and payable to the incumbent of the church of Beaumont only."

Two oak trees originally marked the site of Mose church but in 1957, a concrete cross was erected by R R Austin of Clacton. At one time, there was a yearly service on the site. I am unsure if this tradition is still upheld. The parish registers survive from 1548 until its demise in 1678.

Location: Just southeast of Old Mose Hall. As already mentioned, a stone monument shows the site of the altar. The two oak trees still survive and are thought to mark the, entrance to the churchyard. Contact the owners of Old Mose Hall before entering the site since signs advise that the property is private and trespassers are prosecuted.

Cross erected in 1959 on the site of Mose church

Mundon
(OS Ref: TL 8797 0265)

Mundon is almost a forgotten parish in the Dengie Hundred; three miles south of Maldon near the B1118, on a creek of the River Blackwater. The church, dedicated to the Virgin Mary, sits alone beside Mundon Hall.

Morant described the church as "... tyled and so is the chancel. The Belfry is framed of timber and plastered; octangular below above four square, boarded and tyled. In it are three bells." In the 1830s, Wright described it simply as "a small ancient building, dedicated to the Virgin Mary."

St Mary's is often described as "a beautiful little church" which it is. It undoubtedly has Norman foundations - built within the moat of Mundon Hall. The building you see today was built of rubble (now coated with plaster) in the 14th century. The chancel was rebuilt early in the 18th century, is 20 by 16 feet and retains its original east and north windows.

The nave is 38 by 20 feet and houses, in the north wall, an early 14th century window with Y-tracery and a blocked doorway. On the south, is a blocked doorway of the 18th century and, further east, a fine Tudor brick window appears. A blocked 16th century archway led to a now demolished chapel.

The wonderful timber north porch has been dated to about 1600 and was described by Hewett as "the finest example of its kind seen in the county."

The characteristic hexagonal timber belfry is by far the most well known part of the church. Worley described it as having "massive beams at the west end, arranged hexagonally, and tapering upwards to the belfry which rests upon it." There were three bells originally housed in the belfry - only one has survived. This is thought to have been cast by John Langhome in about 1400.

The late Norman font was originally square. It had the corners removed in a later century when this became the fashion but it has since been removed from the church. The words "Behold the Lamb of God" appear on the chancel arch.

St Mary's appears to have thrived during the early Tudor years, having many of its notable features built then; belfry, north porch and chapel. However, by 1684 it was in a poor state of repair and was not renovated until early in the next century. As time passed, the population drifted away from the coast and fewer parishioners joined the services.

By 1950, despite having recently been repaired, St Mary's was left to rot. By the late 1950s the roof and some of the walls was badly damaged. When Mundon was joined with Latchingdon, it looked as if the church would be demolished. Scarfe visited it in 1967 and described it as "overgrown with elder and brambles, the chancel wide open on the north side, dangerously ruinous." However, in 1975 a year after the parish had been transferred to St Mary's, Maldon, the church was taken into the care of the Friends of Friendless Churches. It was extensively repaired and its future now

Mundon church interior

looks secure. Let us hope we can continue to enjoy this church for many years to come.

Location: Take the Mundon Road south from Maldon to Mundon, left into New Hall Lane and then right into Vicarage Lane. The church is hidden beside Mundon Hall.

Mundon church, 1927

Northwood
(OS Ref: TL 8012 3920?)

Information on the parish of Northwood is almost non-existent. From my researches
in the Essex Record Office, I have been unable to uncover any information as to its
history, appearance, demise or location. The only evidence I have for its existence is
its place on the Essex Parish Map. Here it lies between the parishes of Little Yeldham,
Castle Hedingham, Gestingthorpe, Belchamp Walter and Belchamp Otten.

While browsing over my OS maps one day, looking for a possible site for this
church, I noticed St Mary Hall sitting right in the middle of these very parishes. As
this is sited nowhere near another church and was probably named for its association
with a building called St Mary's I suspect this area is a likely candidate for the
location. The church was perhaps behind the hall - possibly near the pond. On the
Chapman and André map of 1777, there is shown a clump of trees called Northey
Wood from which the parish got its name!

Location: St Mary Hall is beside a narrow road halfway between Little Yeldham and
Belchamp Otten. The owners advised me that there is nothing to see in relation to the
church on their land.

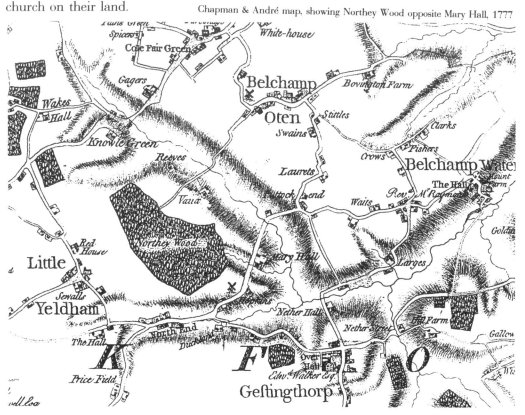

Chapman & André map, showing Northey Wood opposite Mary Hall, 1777

Pitsea
(OS Ref: TQ 7384 8776)

St Michael's, Pitsea, sits on a hill overlooking a housing estate and the town's main road. As a child, I remember this church still in use by the parish but now it has fallen into decay. A wire fence encloses the overgrown grounds. The building presents, a sorry sight; its walls are crumbling and wind whistles through the roof. A sign on the tower declares "Keep Out - You have been warned."

Morant described it in the 1760s as "dedicated to St Michael, stands high; and so do most of those which are dedicated to that Archangel. From thence is a delightful prospect. It is of one pace with the chancel, tiled. A Tower, of stone, with a spire shingled, contains 3 Bells."

H W King tells us that in 1848 St Michael's was protected from its "remarkably exposed situation" by "a clump of ancient elms." He visited again in 1864 and noted that it was "a small structure in the late Perpendicular style." King wrote that the south side and east end of the chancel had been rebuilt in a "most barbarous style, of brick." He mentions that there was no window on the south of the chancel - but a "very late square headed window" on the north. There was a blocked plain pointed arch north doorway in the nave as well as two windows. Two square headed windows occupied the south wall of the nave.

King mentions that the south porch was brick built and "of Elizabethan character." He further explains that it had a "Tudor headed entrance and stepped buttresses set on the angles. On the west side of it is a fireplace with wide chimney cutting off one of the windows." He stated that it looked as if the fireplace had long been disused. The pews had bench ends which King described as "possibly... from the time of Henry 8th."

The west tower was built in the 16th century and the RCHM describes it as "ashlar faced with dressings of Reigate stone." It is 8 feet square and built in three stages with an embattled parapet and gargoyles at each corner. Mason's marks were once visible on the east doorway - dated to the early 16th century. Inside were three bells - the oldest made by Henry Jordan in the 15th century, the others made by John Wilnar in 1636.

A brass was once visible in the chancel to Elizabeth (Rayne) wife of John Purlenant and dated 1588. I have been unable to find out where this is now. It may have been stolen. There was once also an early 16th century plain octagonal font. An Elizabethan chalice of 1568 and a paten (bearing the arms of Sir Thomas Moyer) of 1692 were also attached to the church, I am unsure as to their present whereabouts.

In about 1869, a fire gutted the church and destroyed much of the chancel, nave and porch. Fortunately, the tower was virtually untouched.

In December, 1870, the vicar sought from the Bishop of Rochester, a faculty to demolish the church with the exception of the tower. He wanted to extend the already

Pitsea church in 1912 ... and today

full churchyard further north. It was estimated that rebuilding would cost £1,100. This sum had already been raised by subscription from the "Patrons, Landowners, occupiers and inhabitants." The chancel, nave and porch were rebuilt in 1871 in Kentish Ragstone to the design of Sir Arthur Bloomfield.

As far as I remember, Pitsea church was still in use in the early 1970s. In the last couple of years, a number of attempts have been made to save it - or at least the tower. In December, 1998, despite valiant attempts by locals trying to keep and restore the building, the nave and chancel were pulled down to about a foot in height. At the time of writing, Christmas, 1998, the tower is about to be restored by the telephone company 'Orange'.

Location: St Michael's is on a hill overlooking the conjunction of the A13 and the A132 at Pitsea roundabout. To get to the church, head towards the railway station and then turn left, down Brackendale Avenue. Turn down St Michael's Avenue, park at the end of this road and walk up to the remains of the church.

Interior of Pitsea church, 1996

Pleshey
(OS Ref TL 6635 1457)

The first church of Pleshey is believed to have been built in the inner precincts of the castle. It is often described as a chapel and I am unsure as to whether it ever had parish status. It was possibly built in about 1180, the same time as the castle, among the other castle buildings: stables, barns, storehouses, workshops, the garrison and armoury. In the late 14th century an inventory was made giving us details of what this early chapel looked like "in the chapel were many elaborate vestments - a blue cope worked with beasts and birds with frets of Poles with arters inscribed, with all freeze of cloth of Cyprus gold embroidered with images, lined with satin."

The chapel must have been a large, splendidly furnished building for its altar had a front "of cloth of Cyprus gold embroidered with ten large images... 44 yards long and 12 yards in depth". Among the long list of seventy-five chapel items on the inventory were "many elaborate vestments for the bishops visiting." In 1558, it was reported that "an old Chappell bylte of pybble robysshe and lyme with some lytle wyndowes of stone in the same" was very decayed. It is thought that this may have been demolished some time around this date. The Commissioners estimated the value of the materials as "thirtee thre pounde fyve shillings & eight pence".

The second church at Pleshey was built some time between 1180 and 1400. It was dedicated to St Mary and was built to the north-west of the castle. Earlier editions of the Ordnance Survey map show the approximate site of this church in the precincts of the Lower Bailey.

Except for a small chapel dedicated to St Nicholas, the church was demolished in about 1394. Eventually, around the mid-1500s, the chapel was also pulled down.

The third church was built in 1394/5 in the grounds of the college at the same time as St Mary's was demolished. A list of those who consented to the rebuilding of the church included many locals but also some important dignitaries such as Humphrey, Duke of Gloucester, and Buckingham, Constable of England. Many parts of the old building of St Mary were re-used in this new structure. The north, south and west arches of the central tower as well as the foundations of the north and south transepts were re-housed. In 1460, Buckingham died at the Battle of Northampton and left money to build a north chapel attached to the church. This was dedicated to the Holy Trinity.

In the mid-16th century, despite the fact that many nobles were buried beneath, John Gate pulled down the chancel in order to raise money. The parishioners grouped together and bought the rest of the church to ensure they were not deprived of a place to worship.

Unfortunately, the church remained ruinous for over a hundred and fifty years. Without a wealthy patron, the population was too poor to rebuild it to its former glory. In 1664, the church is described as having 'fallen down'. Bishop Compson built a small brick church on the site of the nave in 1708. Until this time, the parish registers had been neglected. The tower and chancel remained dilapidated.

Finally, in the early 18th century a wealthy landowner, Sir William Jolly purchased the manor. In 1725 his heirs rebuilt the chapel, repaired the tower, recast the old bells and added two new ones. And so, for 140 years the church stood thus, until in 1868 the Holy Trinity was almost entirely rebuilt. This incorporated the arches of the central tower and probably the foundations of the north and south transepts of the original St Mary's church. The rest was a completely new building.

Margaret Avery reported in 1981 that "until comparatively recent times... the foundation of St Nicholas could be seen." Unfortunately, this is no longer the case.

Location: Visitors to the site of Pleshey Castle should make an appointment with the owners of the nearby Hall. There is little indication of the original chapel at ground level. The site of St Mary's is in a private field. When I last visited, there were pigs in the field. Again, there is no indication of the precise site of the church and no stone has been found recently.

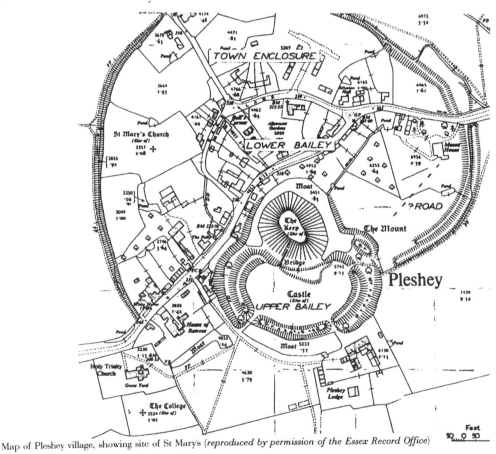

Map of Pleshey village, showing site of St Mary's (*reproduced by permission of the Essex Record Office*)

Shopland
(OS Ref: TQ 8989 8833)

St Mary Magdalen, in the parish of Shopland, stood near the end of Shopland Hall Lane, just three miles north-east of Southend-on-Sea. Shopland's parish church was Norman in origin and measured about 60 feet by 19 feet. Built principally in the 12th century, like most other churches it saw numerous alterations over the next three centuries. During this period the chancel was rebuilt, widened, a porch was added, and a bell turret was built. The fabric of the church was rubble covered with cement and roughcast. It had the traditional limestone dressing.

The Norman chancel was 21 feet by 19 feet. It was rebuilt and widened in the 13th or 14th century. A couple of 14th century windows were added as well as a 15th century north doorway. The east window combined modern and 14th century work. A 14th century piscina was in residence along with a sedile. The nave was 39 feet by 19 feet, and was built early in the 12th century. There were two small early 12th century windows (that in the south wall was later blocked) and four further windows; two 14th century; one 15th century and one Victorian. The timber south porch was a fine example of 15th century craftsmanship. The roofs of both the chancel and nave dated back to the 14th or 15th century. The bell turret was added in the 16th century and housed just one bell made by Peter Hawkes in 1608.

At the time of the Royal Commission's investigations in the 1920s, mediæval glass was present in the east window and mediæval tiles were visible in the nave floor. A fine brass to Thomas Stapel "in armour with pointed bascinet, camail ... and cinquefoiled crocheted canopy and shields" could be seen in the nave partially obscured by some pews. He was Sergeant at Arms to King Edward III and fought at Crécy and Poitiers, dying in 1371.

When H W King visited St Mary Magdalene in 1847, he found no arch separating the chancel from the nave: this is unusual for a Norman church. Perhaps it was demolished when the chancel was widened in the 13th or 14th century. King also describes a priest's door on the north side of the chancel and a piscina with a rose basin. On his second visit in 1863, he found a new west window had been installed in the Decorated style. This would indicate that St Mary's was still well used at this time.

The church began to deteriorate some time after this. In 1906, the walls were repaired at a cost of £43 10s. In August, 1928, a complete restoration began. All the materials were donated by friends of the church. Long hidden Norman windows and doors were reopened and new furniture was installed. The old box pews were removed. The entire church was re-floored, replastered and white washed.

Early in 1930, gales after evensong inflicted considerable damage to the church roof. The damage was repaired, but just four years later gales wrought further severe damage. Once again, repairs were paid for privately.

By 1933 the parish of Shopland, having very few inhabitants (and no shop despite its name), was split between Southend-on-Sea and Sutton. The church's condition had now become desperate, in 1936 the chancel was said to be in a 'disgraceful state'. During World War II, a land mine compounded the deterioration when it exploded 150 yards from the structure causing damage to the east window and the roof. Further bombing in the vicinity continued the destruction.

Vandalism and dwindling congregations finally forced the church to close. On 6th September, 1940, St Mary's saw its last service: a christening. In 1957, it was finally demolished. Its ancient treasures were dispersed to churches around the county. The 15th century timber porch was removed to St Thomas, Bradwell-on-Sea. The square 13th century font, described in much detail by the Royal Commission, found its way to nearby Canewdon. Peter Hawkins' bell went to St Chad's in Vange.

Thomas Stapel's brass made the short journey a mile northwest to Sutton, as did a late 17th century mural monument to Charles Tyrell which had formally resided in the chancel.

The church's former position is evident as a sunken rectangular clearing between many remaining headstones. The graveyard contains the remains of the Benton family, including the Rochford Hundred's renowned local historian, Philip Benton. Local badgers, it appears, regularly excavate his grave. The site of St Mary Magdalene lies just a few miles north of the busy seaside town of Southend-on-sea, yet it could be a world away. Each summer the rector of nearby Sutton holds an open-air service in memory of the families that lived in the parish and those who are buried in the churchyard.

Location: St Mary Magdalen was near the end of Shopland Hall Lane about three miles north-east of Southend-on-Sea. The site is freely accessible to the public.

Sketch of Shopland church
by H W King, 1848

Snoreham
(OS Ref: TQ 8850 9967)

The ancient parish of Snoreham is now combined with that of Latchingdon and is about two and a half miles from Cold Norton. The church was dedicated to St Peter and stood just south of Snoreham Hall.

It is thought to have been erected by some of the noble family of Grey of Wilton in the 14th century. However, I have been unable to unearth the exact age of the building; the material used in its structure or any indication of its layout. Hopefully, the site will be scheduled for an archæological dig one day.

It is difficult to say for certain when the church was finally abandoned and demolished. Most sources merely state that it decayed 'several centuries' ago. H W King guessed that this was in the mid-1500s. However, many have estimated abandonment as late as around 1656. At this time parishioners were being petitioned to contribute towards repairs at Latchingdon St Michael.

Morant described the church in the 1760s as "...quite ruinous, there being only some small remains of it near the Hall-yard. The inhabitants resort to Latchingdon church as being the nearest, and these are baptised and buried, and contribute to all parochial duties." Cox said that the church "stood in the stockyard at the Hall." Again, mention is made that there were still some fragments of remains at the site in the mid-1800s.

Each year a sermon was preached under a tree at the approximate site of the church. This tradition was kept up intermittently for many years - a few services even taking place in this century in the garden of the Hall.

Location: The site of the church is in a field to the south-east of Snoreham Hall. The precise position of it is difficult to ascertain although the approximate site is marked on the early Ordnance Survey maps. The site is on private land and it is therefore advisable to make a prior appointment with the owner of Snoreham Hall.

Site of Snoreham church (*reproduced from the 1897 Ordnance Survey*)

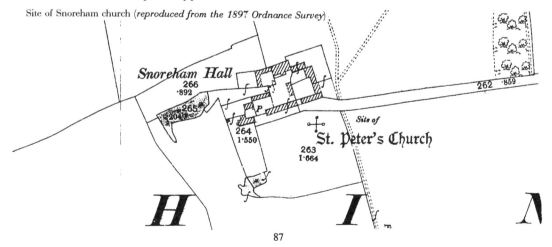

Stanway All Saints
(OS Ref: TL 9531 2210)

Before the 14th century, Stanway was divided into two separate parishes. Little Stanway was in the north of the present parish and was served by the church of St Albright. Great Stanway was in the south, beside Stanway Hall and encompassed All Saints Church. By the end of the 14th century, the church of St Albright's was known as a chapel to "All Saints" and the parishes appear to have been joined.

All Saints originally consisted of a nave, chancel, west tower and north aisle. The walls are made of pebble and ragstone rubble and include a large amount of red tiles and brick - probably re-used from a local Roman Villa.

The nave is just over 39 ! y 16 feet. Its south wall is 3 feet thick. The chancel was demolished in the 17th century when the 14th century chancel arch was blocked up. The west tower is made up of alternate courses of brick and flint. It is by far the most impressive feature of the church. It is 9 feet square and with walls 3½ feet thick. Built in three stages in the 14th century it includes an embattled parapet. If you can gain access, the tower arch is most interesting and best viewed from inside the nave.

Most of the original church was built in the 14th century. Said to have been in a poor state of repair by the time of the Reformation, it was restored by Sir John Swinerton early in the 17th century, when a porch was added to the side of the north aisle. Sir Symond D'Ewes wrote in 1633 of two ancient graves he found in the chancel with the brasses removed. These are no longer visible as the chancel has not survived.

Unfortunately, All Saints was not to remain in good condition for very long. During the civil wars (1642-49), and most likely, during the siege of Colchester (1648), the Parliamentarian troops appear to have taken both lead and timber from the roof. The church, now open to the elements, deteriorated rapidly after this.

Although attempts were made to restore it during the reign of Charles II, it was not long before St Albright's appears to have taken over as the parish church. While All Saints continued its decline, St Albright's was widened and lengthened in 1826. In 1880, it was completely restored by Sir Gilbert Scott. This restoration work included the incorporation of a south aisle from the ancient church of St Runwald's, Colchester, which was demolished in 1878 (see page 22). A new church dedicated to All Saints was built in brick in 1845 on the Maldon Road.

Nowadays, All Saints Church is passed by largely unnoticed, by thousands of visitors to Colchester Zoo. Some years ago, the zoo encompassed the church building. Rather fittingly at that point, vultures looked on to the building. However, now the zoo entrance proper is further south.

Location: The ruins are beside the Maldon Road inside the grounds of Colchester Zoo. Permission to view the church must be sought from the zoo owners. Entry inside the ruin is very restricted due to its dangerous condition.

Exterior and interior of All Saints, Stanway, 1995

Steeple
(OS Ref: TL 9292 0285)

The small village of Steeple is approximately three miles from Southminster. The old church of St Lawrence and All Saints lay about 150 yards south of Steeple Hall. It is believed that a church stood on this original site from Saxon times. The original church declined over a period of many years and by 1564, the wardens described the chancel as clean down.' The infamous chancellor, Richard Rich, owned the benefice but appears to have done nothing to instigate repairs.

In the 1830s, Wright describes the church as "an old building of mean appearance." In the previous century, Morant had found the chancel "in ruins." He also noted that "at the west end, in a wooden frame boarded and tyled, are 2 Bells."

In 1872 H W King described St Lawrence standing "in a singularly isolated situation on very low ground in the midst of a marsh or meadow a quarter of a mile from the village which, is, on rising ground ... it has been ... remorselessly and cruelly defaced. Only the nave remains and this is small... Salmon does not mention [it being ruinous] in 1740, therefore presumably it was then used. The foundations are pretty well defined at this day."

King believed that "its destruction would save the cost of all future reparation" and indeed, it lasted only ten years after his viewing. He remarked that the vicar and parishioners closed up the end of the nave with red brick in the 18th century. He could find no existence of a tower.

King lamented that "very little ... of the original fabric remains: the north wall is externally of modern brickwork, and the west end has been entirely rebuilt of brick up to the gable which is of weather-boarding.

The ancient buttress remains at the west end, the rest [are] reparations of brickwork. The south doorway is pointed, of the Perpendicular period, the dripstone terminating with corbel heads defaced. There are two windows in the south of Early Perpendicular work, consisting of two acutely pointed cinquefoil cusped lights, and a small single light of debased Perpendicular work deeply set with rather widely splayed jambs which may possibly be an insertion in a Norman opening. There is one modern and barbarous window in the north wall."

He continues "There is a flat plastered ceiling but there are some remains of 15th century timber work at the west end including an arched principal, and on the north side some panelling of Jacobean character.

The Bell is inaccessible but appears to hang in the roof over the ceiling and the sound to be omitted by a lattice in the west gable.... The north door is blocked but the old dripstone remains. There is a porch on the south side which retains some of the old timber framing."

King then went on to describe something "which represents the font, but is not a font." This consisted "of a brick pedestal on the top of which is fixed the base of the old font upside down, in which are worked the bases of 4 small shafts denoting that it was apparently Early English. A small hole through which the chain pipe passed represents the basin, but Holy Baptism is obviously here performed not with water poured into the font, but from a small basin set upon this unsightly pedestal."

In 1882, F Chancellor (who designed Ford End and Pleshey churches) built the new Steeple church 600 yards to the east, beside the main road, in the middle of the village. Much of the material from the old church was incorporated into this new structure. It was designed in the Early English style and built with many different types of stone. Pevsner accused the builder of having "indulged in an orgy of mixing into his brown stone walls bricks entirely at random and in all directions." Viewing the church today one can certainly see Pevsner's point.

The doorway and one of the windows from the old church were re-used. The octagonal font bowl that had long resided in the former churchyard was brought to the new. In the west wall of the vestry are two 12th century head-stops. In the north wall is a late 14th century window.

The late 14th century south doorway was also re-used.

The remains of the old church were obviously demolished at about the same time as the replacement was built. Today, the original site lies in a clump of trees, peppered with badger's sets. Odd pieces of rubble mark out the places where the nave and chancel must have stood. Many gravestones remain.

Location: The site of the church is visible from the farm that encompasses Steeple Hall. It is situated in a copse, in a field to the south of the Hall. The site lies beside a public footpath, fenced off with barbed wire. It is advisable to check with the Hall before paying a visit.

A sketch of
Steeple old
church, 1883

Theydon Bois
(OS Ref: TQ 4631 9795)

The original church of Theydon Bois was dedicated to St Mary. However, the *Victoria County History* suggests it may once have been dedicated to St Botolph. It stood halfway between Theydon and Abridge on the Abridge Road, next to the present Theydon Hall.

The first church contained many Norman features and was probably built in the 12th century. It consisted of a nave, chancel, south porch, and a western wooden bell turret. A single-light window and a door were situated in the chancel. The nave contained two single-light windows and two blocked openings. Morant described it as being "of one pace with the Chancel, and tyled. A little wooden turret, with a spire shingled, contains 3 Bells."

In 1770, and again in 1819, it was said, that there were no monuments or inscriptions in the church. This is rather strange as two monuments from the old church are preserved in the replacement building.

On 12 June, 1843, in the vestry of the old church, it was decided that a replacement church should be built "in a new central site of the parish, in lieu of the present incommodiously situated parish church."

The builder, Mr Smith, estimated the rebuilding work would cost £1,310. It was intended that the old church should, be demolished and some of these materials incorporated into the new building. This was consecrated at a special ceremony conducted by the Bishop of London on 5 June, 1844. It consisted of a chancel, nave and west tower. The actual cost of the new church was £2,231, rather more than the original estimate. The old materials were sold for just £78.

Three bells were brought from the old church; one of about 1460 and one dated 1567; the smallest was recast in 1843. Several hatchments were also transported including four to the Wild family of Theydon Hall and a royal coat of arms of James I dated 1618 (one of only four surviving in England). Some 19th century monuments were removed to the new church. The original communion plate and font were both lost with the church.

Just four years after this second church was finished, cracks appeared in the walls. It was found to have insufficient foundations. A meeting was held in the new vestry to discuss the "unsatisfactory condition of the parish church." It was decided. that another church should be built on this same site to the design of Samuel Smirke. He had recently finished St John's at Loughton.

This second replacement church was built of brick and stone in the Early English style and consecrated on 5 February, 1851. The cost of the new building was approximately £2,000 and consisted of a nave, chancel, north vestry and large western tower with a spire.

A few years ago, some old tombstones were said to stand in the old churchyard.

These appear to have been removed. Only a plaque remains, in the grounds of Theydon Hall, stating the church's position and giving a few details of the last surviving gravestones.

Location: The first church was sited beside Theydon Hall, which is now nestled within sight of the M11 off the B172, Abridge Road. A black marble plaque indicates its original position, but other than this, there is no view of the original site as it is in the walled grounds of Theydon Hall.

Commemorative
plaque on the site of
Theydon Bois
old church

Theydon Bois
old church, 1814

Thunderley
(OS Ref: TL 5606 3583)

Thunderley was once a distinct parish in the north-west of Essex in the Hundred of Uttlesford, just two miles south-east of Saffron Walden. The church, of which there is no known depiction or description was sited approximately 300 yards south of Thunderley Hall. Early editions of the Ordnance Survey map show the precise position of the site. Morant described it as being "on the left side of the road leading from Thaxted to Walden." The hall is still there but much altered. The hamlet, however, is no longer found on the Ordnance Survey map.

About 66 feet in length, the church is thought to have been aisleless and to consist of a nave, chancel, west tower and south porch.

Thunderley has been described as the earliest redundant church in Essex having been 'lost' in the early 15th century. It is believed that the Black Death devastated Thunderley and the surrounding area so badly in the 14th century that the church and the hall were abandoned. Neither the church nor the hall was used for many years. This is possibly the reason why Thunderley church became ruinous and was eventually demolished. In 1425, the ancient parish of Thunderley was united with the nearby parish of Wimbish and the church destroyed. Parts of the church were saved and incorporated in Wimbish church where 'Thunderley aisle' and also a chapel of the same name exist. It is thought that Thunderley stone was used here to mend an already existing aisle and chapel.

Thunderley Hall houses three ancient doors. One of these is, I am sure, one of the entrance doors to the church. It is a fine looking door with much ancient studding. Two other two doors in the Hall are also very possibly from this church.

In the 1760s Morant could detect no sign of Thunderley church or churchyard. The area was now under farmland. Cox, however, a hundred years ago, tells us that 'the foundations of its parish church can still be traced'. Worley also noted that there were still "some faint traces of its foundations on the road to Thaxted." Indeed, the Royal Commission in the 1920s described the site as being "indicated by a sinking in the turf."

Today there is nothing to tell the casual observer where the church once stood. Some years ago, the hollow was filled in to facilitate ploughing. Many years ago a key was found on the site and is thought to have been from the church. There are still odd pieces of stone, flint and tiles on the site of the church - despite 500 years of tilling and ploughing!

Location: The land lies 300 metres from Thunderley Hall, just south of the pond, on the west of the road between, Thaxted and Saffron Walden. If you wish to visit the site, the tenant farmers of Thunderley Hall should be contacted first. Visitors are preferred after the harvest has been gathered.

One of the doors in Thunderley Hall
believed to have come from the church

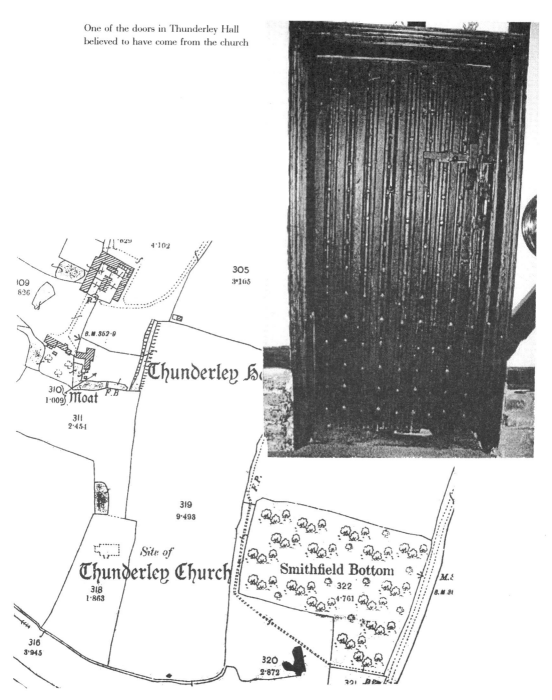

Site of Thunderley old church
(*reproduced from the 1897 Ordnance Survey*)

Virley
(OS Ref: TL 9495 1375)

In the grounds of the old rectory, lie the remains of the Parish Church of St Mary, Virley. This tiny church, once famous by featuring in Sabine Baring-Gould's 1880 novel *Mehalah*, now lies in ruin. A mere stone's throw across the creek, its sister church Salcott sits proud, seemingly untouched by the ravages of time. (Salcott was, however, badly damaged in the 1884 earthquake and has been largely reconstructed.)

Salmon's *History of Essex* stated that in 1740 St Mary's "steeple is fallen down." By the 1760s, the church had deteriorated further. Morant described the church as: "very small and tiled. The Tower being fallen down, there is only a small timber enclosure which contains 1 bell."

In *Mehalah*, Baring-Gould, while rector of East Mersea, created a vivid and extensive picture of what the church looked like around 1870. He describes the exterior as "a small hunchbacked edifice in the last stages of dilapidation, in a graveyard unhedged, unwalled; the church is scrambled over by ivy, with lattice windows bulged in by the violence of the gales, and a bellcot leaning on one side like a drunkard."

He describes the interior as "even less decent. It possessed but one bell ... Virley Church is not bigger than a stable that consists of two stalls and a loose box, whereas the loose box represents the chancel. [The] Church possessed one respectable feature, a massive chancel arch but that gaped and the pillars slouched back against the wall in the attitude of the Virley men in the village street waiting to insult the women as they went by ... On either side of the east window hung one table of the commandments but a village humorist had erased all the 'nots' in the decalogue; and it cannot be denied that the parishioners conscientiously did their utmost to fulfil the letter of the law thus altered."

He continues "...the chancel of Virley had fallen, and had been rebuilt with timber and bricks on the old walls left to the height of two feet above the floor. As the old walls were four feet thick, and the new walls only the thickness of one brick, the chancel was provided with a low seat all round it, like the cancello of an ancient basilica."

He describes the altar as "a deal table, much worm-eaten, with a box beneath it. The altar possessed no cover save the red cotton pocket-handkerchief of the curate cast occasionally across it. The box contained the battered Communion plate, an ironmoulded surplice with high collar, a register-book, the pages glued together with damp, and a brush and pan. The Communion rails had rotted at the bottom; and when there was a Communion the clerk had to caution the kneelers not to lean against the balustrade, lest they should be precipitated upon the sanctuary floor ... the floor, in the midst, before the altar, had been eaten through by rats, emerging from an old grave and exposed below gnawed and mouldy bones a foot beneath the boards."

The ruins of Virley church today
Site of Virley church from Chapman & Andrés 1777 map

As you can tell from this evocative description, the church was less than perfect at this time! It was clear that unless some serious money was spent on restoring the church it would remain ruined for the rest of its days. The earthquake of 1884, however, sealed its fate. Resultant damage meant the roof had to be removed. The vestry minutes of 29 December, 1892, record that a petition was made to the Lord Bishop of the Diocese.

This asked that the Parish Church of Salcott be considered as the Parish Church of the united parishes of Salcott and Virley. It was further required that the Parish Church of St Mary Virley (which had been ruined for the last twelve years) be "suffered to remain a ruin." And that; "the sum of £124.10, intended for the Restoration of the chancel of Virley church, be used toward the building of a chancel to Salcott church."

The petition added that there were no "tombstones, monuments, tablets or monumental inscriptions" in the old churchyard at Virley.

Further that there were "no sums of money or other property held by anybody or person or persons in trust for the maintenance, repair or insurance" of the parish church of Virley.

Today, Roman tiles can be seen in the parts of the walls of Virley that remain. It appears that many times the walls were buttressed, sometimes in a crude manner; these battered remnants live on. The most interesting architectural vestige is the chancel arch - built in the Transitional style of the early 13th century. The walls are of mixed rubble with some Roman bricks. The chancel and nave were built probably early in the 13th century, but later windows may indicate partial rebuilding of both parts.

The chancel was 20½ feet by 14½ feet, but now has the east and south walls ruined to floor level. The north wall had two 15th century windows and included some 17th century brick. The nave was originally 19 feet wide and is now of an indeterminate length. The window in the north wall was from the 14th century, though little remains.

Location: The ruins can be found approximately two miles north-east of Tolleshunt D'Arcy just off the B1026. The church is on the land of the old rectory and it is therefore advisable to ask the owner of this house for permission to view it. It is a small ruin - quite unremarkable except for its relationship with *Mehalah* and the vision of it left by Baring-Gould.

Walton on the Naze
(OS Ref c.TM 257 217)

Walton le Soke (to give it its ecclesiastical title) has possessed a church since the 13th century and possibly earlier. The original mediæval building was "small, had two aisles, [and] the chancel [was of] one pace." It also had a steeple at the western end. The living of Walton was united with nearby Kirby-le-Soken from 1630, Walton being just a small village at this time.

Around 1710, Holman describes the church as: "pleasantly situated on the seaside which in course of time has mightily gained on the terra firma and in a few years must wash away this church." He went on to describe the steeple as: "a fair one that served for a sea mast which with part of the body of the church is fallen down. Though it stands high yet the walls and floor seem moist by reason of the salt water being so high... and must in a little time wash it away as it has a great part of this parish."

It is thought that an extension was made to the church sometime after 1730. However, by 1768, Walton's church was starting to decay. Morant describes the church as "now in ruins." The sea was only 150 yards from its eastern end. In an engraving of 1777, the tower has already collapsed due to the instability of the surrounding land. The roof was also in a deplorable state of repair. At this time, smugglers were using it to stash their hoards. Services were only occasional but continued until its demise. It was during such a service in 1789 that the roof finally collapsed.

Since the sea was now lapping at the foundations, reluctantly the church was largely abandoned. However it stood for a further nine years, during which time some weddings were held in the porch before the structure finally succumbed to the sea in 1798. Some time after this, it was said that coffins continued to be washed up onto the shore. The wood was apparently used by the villagers to repair furniture. By the time Wright wrote about Walton's church in 1831, the sea had advanced several hundred feet beyond the place where it stood. Today the site of the church is a mile or so out to sea on the west rocks.

Walton church had distinguished connections. The lands around the church belonged to St Paul's Cathedral, London. The cathedral contains a memorial to the church in the form of a prebendal stall known as *prebenda consumpta per mare* (eaten up by the sea).

At very low tide, it is said that the church foundations have been glimpsed far from the shore. Locals claim to have heard the church bells toll, warning the town of impending sea storms. This is romantic but unlikely since the bells, along with the parish registers (dating from 1672), were recovered from the church before its submersion.

In 1804, a new church, dedicated to All Saints, was built. It was a small red brick building with a square bell tower. This church was restored and enlarged in 1832 and again in 1835. With the sudden explosion of seaside resorts in the Victorian era, the church was inadequate for Walton's growing population. It was therefore substantially rebuilt in 1873. Part of the nave, a new chancel and a south aisle were added. The fine tower was not completed until 1895. This is essentially the church to be seen in Walton today.

Location: Three churches have been described above. The original is some distance off the present coast. If you are still keen to visit, the local history society has information on its precise whereabouts; but take your snorkel!

Etching of Walton on the Naze old church, 1787

Wenden Lofts
(OS Ref: TL 4640 3873)

Four miles from Audley End and Saffron Walden, St Dunstan's is now set beside the
new Lofts Hall. This Hall, built in a neo-Georgian style, replaced an Elizabethan
house of brick constructed in about 1580 which was destroyed in 1965. The parish
derived its name from the ancient 13th century Loughs family.

In the 1760s, Morant described St Dunstan's as "a small low building, but with a
good prospect over the country." Wright went on to describe it in the 1830s as "a low
ancient building, in good repair."

The church contained a 15th century brass with effigies, dedicated to William
Lucas, Katherine Lucas (c 1456) and their four sons and four daughters. One son
wears the dress and holds the crosier of a prior or abbot. The current whereabouts
of this brass is not known. Bertram's *Lost Brasses* says that it was stolen from the
church in 1940.

The building is of Norman origin but was reconstructed in 1845 in the 15th
century style. Very little of the original structure is left and I have been unable to find
any descriptions or sketches of it other than of the type quoted above. The beautiful
Norman Romanesque doorway is still in existence on the south side. Worley describes
"its bold rounded arch, with chevron moulding, resting on circular shafts with slightly
carved caps."

During the rebuilding three bells were hung in the tower. A three-decker pulpit
remained in 1940 but is no longer in evidence. Perhaps it was removed to a nearby
attended church. Some 18th century stained glass remained in the windows. This
consisted of a sundial and Jacob's ladder with a symbolic snail. Also included were "a
figure of charity, scenes of the Nativity, the Crucifixion, and a group of armed men
with a camel." This glass was moved to Elmdon when Wenden was declared
redundant.

St Dunstan's was partially demolished in 1958, later declared redundant and is
now privately owned by the occupant of the Hall. The Norman doorway is the only
protected part of the church.

A wall-monument tells of the Wilkes family who worshipped there for a century.
One member bore the entire cost of rebuilding the church. The interior of the church
is in a serious state of disrepair. The nave is currently occupied by an old pram and
a small rowing boat. The rest of the floor is strewn with stone and debris.

Location: The church lies down a private road, next door to Wenden Hall. Permission
must be gained from the Hall owner, particularly to visit the interior. The Norman
doorway is well worth the effort.

Wenden Lofts church today

The fine south doorway of Wenden Lofts

The interior of Wenden Lofts (complete with boat & pram!)

West Horndon
(OS Ref: TQ 624 897)

The parish church of St Nicholas, West Horndon, stood just south of West Horndon Hall. There were three bells housed within its tower.

Walker depicted the church pictorially on a map of 1598. This indicates a nave and chancel with an embattled west tower and a south porch.

Although maps of this era were renowned for giving 'stylised' views of churches, Walker is known as a careful cartographer. The picture can therefore be assumed to be a fairly accurate representation of the church.

By the 18th century the church of West Horndon and that of nearby Ingrave (see page ??) had grown quite ruinous. An Act of Parliament was therefore obtained for uniting the two parishes in 1735.

The original churches were demolished and a new red brick structure was built in that year at the bequest of Lord Petre. It stands beside the main road to Brentwood, halfway between the two church sites.

Two brasses from the old church of West Horndon were housed in the new building. One commemorated Margaret Fitz-Lewis c. 1450. The other was dedicated to John Fitz-Lewis (c 1500) and his four wives.

None of the old church's original structure appears to have been used in the new.

Incidentally, West Horndon's current parish church is of interest, being a prefabricated building of the early 1950s, now possibly unique as a place of worship.

Location: The site of the old church of West Horndon is quite difficult to locate for the casual observer. The church was only a few yards south of West Horndon Hall. The former site of the Hall is shown approximately on the pathfinder series of the Ordnance Survey maps. From comparing this with older maps, the site of the church Was in a fenced-off area, in a field, just below the rise of the hill to the east of Jury Hill. (I gained access via a lane off the A127.)

The last remains of West Horndon church

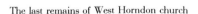

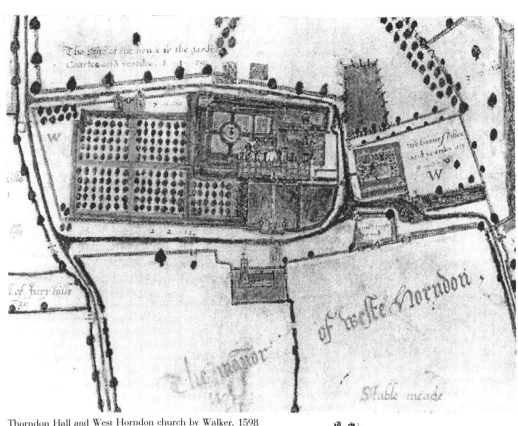

Thorndon Hall and West Horndon church by Walker, 1598
Site of West Horndon church (*reproduced from the 1897 Ordnance Survey*)

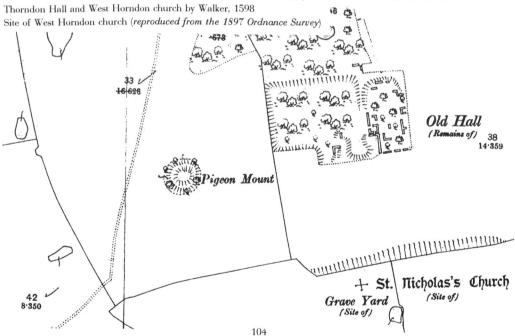

West Lee (or West Ley)
(OS Ref:TQ 6850 8694?)

The church of West Lee stood near Westley Hall between the parishes of Vange and Langdon Hills. Unfortunately, no description of the make-up or features of this church survives. We do not even know to whom it was dedicated.

The impoverished condition of the church was noted as early as the 12th century. In her book, *A Pictorial History of Basildon*, Jessie Payne says: "When in 1297, the Dean visited the church he found it in a ruinous condition. Cattle were feeding in the churchyard, as the fence was broken. The wooden font leaked, the nave windows were unglazed and there was no bell."

In the early 1400s, the church was again reported as being in a poor state of repair. Its future was uncertain since the income had become so small that no minister was willing to accept the living. As patrons, the Dean and Chapter of St Paul's deplored its neglected condition. The Bishop was eventually asked to join it to the neighbouring parish church of Langdon Hills. On 22 July, 1432, the Bishop gave permission for the two parishes of Langdon Hills and West Lee to be united. The church of West Lee was then demolished.

The *Victoria County History* records that the church of Langdon was so close to West Lee that the parishioners could easily attend this church. It also mentions financial considerations for the demolition and amalgamation: "through the malice of men, the mortality of cattle, and the neglect of tillage, [the church] had become so impoverished that the rector was not able to maintain such convenient hospitality as was required, or to keep the chancel and manse and buildings in due repair."

It was therefore decided that the rector of Langdon was "to say mass once a year in the church of West Lee at the feast of its dedication." Even this cannot have been easy, as West Lee Church was described as "*derelicta, desolata, et inofficiata*"

The original site of the church is open to some speculation. Local tradition has it that timbers from the old church were incorporated into the old barn south of West Lee Hall. The main timber within this barn does indeed appear ancient. Just to the south of this barn lies a field with many lumps and bumps as well as a flatter area. This is very likely the site of West Lee's ancient church.

Location: To the south of West Lee Hall, lie a couple of barns (perhaps containing timbers from the church.) Behind these lies a field. It is believed that the site of the church was here.

Timbers in nearby barn, purported to come from West Lee church

Chapman & André map showing West Lee, 1777

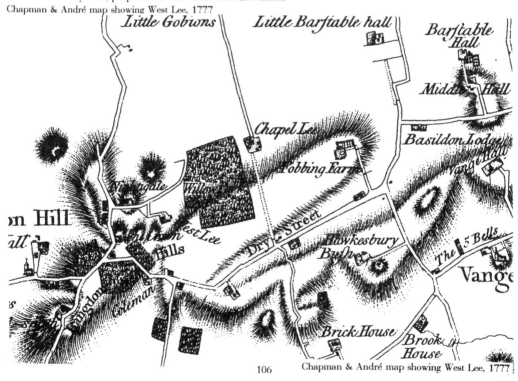

Chapman & André map showing West Lee, 1777

Wickham Bishops
(OS Ref - TL8248 1119)

The old parish church of Wickham Bishops is currently a ruin and can be found a mile southwest of the village centre and three miles north of Maldon. It stands in the middle of fields next to an old cottage, close by the bridge over the dismantled Witham to Maldon railway line. There is some contention as to whether this church was originally dedicated to St Peter or, as some sources would have it, St Bartholomew. The Ordnance Survey and Rodwell both refer to it as St Peter's.

It consists of a chancel, nave, south porch and south vestry. Rodwell believes it to be a Saxon or Saxo-Norman church. The walls are of stone, flint-rubble and boulder clay. Covered with plaster in the past, large parts of the walls are now laid bare, uncovering the true fabric of the church. It is dressed with limestone as are many Essex churches.

The chancel is 19 feet by 13 feet and is late 11th century in date - possibly earlier. There may have been a chancel arch separating the chancel from the nave but this has not survived. Roman bricks were incorporated into the corners of the chancel. Roman tiles were set round a doorway. All the windows are 14th century. The nave is 39 feet by 19 feet and is of a similar date. The nave windows are also of the 14th century but with little surviving original tracery. There is a 15th century south doorway, which replaced a now blocked 11th century one. There is also a west doorway of the 15th century. The south porch is of red brick, built in the 16th century with later repairs.

The 15th century roof is a very fine example of its type. The tie beams of the nave are of particular interest and the plastered timber framing supporting the bell turret is visible at the west end. (Some of this plaster has fallen off giving a better view of this timberwork.)

Holman says that in the early 1700s "The church is small, church and chancel of one pace tiled, a shaft shingled, one bell. It stands down in the fields a considerable distance from the road and from the Hall." He also describes the glass in the church, none of which survives. A brass is mentioned, to Henry Hebylthwayte dated 26th February, 1516. Possibly, this survives in a nearby church. The church's old chest was moved to the replacement church. The octagonal font appears in the Royal Commission's photos and is described as mid-15th century. It is not known what became of it.

A grand new church by Ewan Christian was built in 1850 in the centre of the village.

Since that date, the old building was allowed to fall into a state of disrepair. Fitch described the ruin evocatively in his *Maldon and the Blackwater:* "The old church ... now disused and fast going to decay, stands down the hill ... and as a picturesque ruin is a familiar, if painful, object to travellers".

The Lady Chapel, Wickham Bishops

End of nave, Wickham Bishops, 1995

In 1969, the rector of Wickham Bishops, Reverend Alistair Gould, tried to get permission to demolish it. However, permission was denied and the 'Friends of Friendless Churches' finally took it into their care. They have saved it from demolition and ensured no further harm comes to the fabric of the building.

On my most recent visit, this fine little church was in a dilapidated condition. The April sunshine lit up the exuberant yellow rapeseed in the fields surrounding it. There are still several gravestones around the structure, principally 19th century but also a few from the 18th century.

A tranquil atmosphere pervades the site, conducive to contemplation: it is one of my favourite ruins. Plans exist to renovate the church. It remains to be seen to what use it will be put. It will then join the thin ranks of re-claimed parish churches of Essex.

Location: Via a small public footpath from Langford road, over the dismantled railway, leading to the church. If you have difficulty finding the ground site, locate the church on the Ordnance Survey map at the above OS reference. At the time of writing, the interior is inaccessible.

St Peter's, Wickham Bishops, 1995

Woodham Walter
(OS Ref: TL 813 065)

The original church of St Michael, Woodham Walter, was very close to the old Hall and was demolished many centuries ago. The Hall itself was pulled down in the last few years of the 17th century - with the cellars remaining a few years longer. Its exact site is shown on some earlier editions of the Ordnance Survey map.

Nothing is known of the look or size of the church. No archæological examination has yet been made of the site. It is said that by the middle of the 16th century, it had become ruined and because of its inconvenient location to the parishioners, it was decided to pull it down and build another nearer the centre of the village. However, at least one local historian is of the opinion that it was more inconvenient to the owner of the land!

Thomas, Earl of Sussex, applied for, and was granted, a licence from Queen Elizabeth in 1562 to build a new church. It was built in red brick and was consecrated on 30th April, 1564. The new church is very unusual in as much as there are very few 16th century churches in Essex.

It is believed that a large part of the interior of the new church was furnished with that of the old. Daphne Kiddle (1977) tells us that "The roof structures over the nave and chancel are fourteenth century." In 1454 Thomas Hawkyn bequeathed the cost of a new aisle on the north side of the old church 'with an honest Chappell on the north side of the Chauncell to be hallowed of our lady and Seint Thomas of Catbury.'

Mrs Kiddle further describes the interior "The pillars between the nave and chancel are most definitely those from the original building for they have been scrawled on and some of the writing has been positively dated as being between 1450 and 1500. The name of William Barton appears written and rewritten in various letter styles, and this at a time in history when few were able to write. His name is found on an item dated 1471 in the Calendar of Patent Rolls when it appears he paid money and was 'pardoned for offenses committed before 6 July'. The roof of the north aisle is also fifteenth century which would indicate that Thomas Hawkyn's north aisle was removed to the new site as was his 'honest chapel' now the vestry."

Wright tells us that "Some fragments of stained glass in the window, are believed to have belonged to the more ancient building."

The 14th century font, in the Perpendicular style, was moved from the old church to the new. Three bells were also removed from the old church and were mentioned in the inventory of the church in 1552. Unfortunately only one of these remains - that made by Giles Jordon, or his son Henry, in about 1470. The other two bells were replaced with later examples - of 1676 and 1713.

Location: Warwick Rodwell stated in 1977 that "St Nicholas lay just to the north of the Hall behind Wilderness Cottage." However, after consultation with a local expert and studying some aerial shots of the area it appears that the site of the church was just west of the Hall - inside the moat. There is nothing to see though on the ground. Perhaps a detailed archæological report will one day be made.

Interior of Woodham Walter church of 1563, incorporating the arches of the former church

Mundon interior

Other Essex Churches no longer in use as Parish Churches

Asheldham, St Lawrence (TL 9789 0127) Diocesan Youth Centre
Built on the site of an ancient settlement, the church you see today is mainly 14th century although it incorporates much reused Roman brick. Since 1986 it has been used at weekends by the Diocesan Youth Centre. It now includes a kitchen and games room.
Not normally open to the public. Apply to churchwarden for access.

Berechurch, St Michael and All Angels (TL 9928 2189) Offices/Chapel
Built in brick about 1500, it houses a superb chapel to the Audley family with an exquisite hammerbeam roof. Viewing by appointment only from the churchwardens.

Bradwell on Sea, St Peter (TM 0310 0817) Chapel
Prior to the building of St Thomas in the village centre (in the 14th century), St Peter's may have been used as the parish church. St Cedd built it, almost entirely of re-used Roman material, in about 654. Originally, it had a west porch and apsidal chancel. It was used as a barn for many years until its uniqueness as an Anglo-Saxon chapel was again realised. Open all reasonable times and well worth the walk.

Braintree, Dedication unknown (c. TL 767 227) Chapel/Church
The original parish church or chapel was to the south-east of Roman Braintree on Chapel Hill. It is thought to have been near the Bishop's Capital - the Manor House. St Michael's replaced this in about 1200. The exact site is open to speculation - no visible remains survive.

Brentwood, St Thomas (TQ 5946 9375) Chapel
St Thomas was a chapel of ease to South Weald as Brentwood did not gain parish status until the 1880s. The old chapel of St Thomas stood on the south side of the High Street and was founded in 1221. It was converted into a school in about 1835 and a new church was built. In 1869, the chapel was all but demolished. All that remains are parts of the north and west wall and most of the west tower. The ruins are permanently open, however, regrettably the tower is not.

Chickney, St Mary (TL 5744 2805) Redundant
A beautiful Saxon church with a 14th century west tower. It was declared redundant many years ago and is now in the hands of the Churches Conservation Trust (CCT). Open most of the time and well worth a visit.

Chignal, St James (TL 6695 0966) Private residence
A small and interesting third Chignal church. Dating from the late 13th century (with flint-rubble and Roman brick walls) it was much restored in the 19th century. It is currently converted to a house.
Not open at any time to the general public.

Colchester, All Saints (TL 9992 2519) Natural History Museum
All Saints has a fine flint west tower, but the rest was much restored in 1861 and there is little else of interest. Open weekdays.

Colchester, Holy Trinity (TL 0061 2510) Museum of rural life
Superb Saxon west tower with a nice tower arch inside. This church was much restored and rebuilt in 1886. This museum was open daily to the general public. However, my past two visits have found it closed.

Colchester, St Martin (TL 9960 2533) Derelict
Disused for many years, it was formerly used by a drama group. It then lay redundant until recently it has been taken over by the Church Conservation Trust. It contains many Roman tiles and bricks - particularly in the tower. Closed at present but will hopefully be open when restoration work is complete.

Colchester, St Giles (TL 9980 2480) Masonic Hall
A small church with nave, chancel and north chapel. The west tower is of wood and weather-boarded. It contains a monument to Sir Charles Lucas and Sir George Lyle shot after the Siege of Colchester (1648). Open to visitors by appointment to the Lodge members.

Colchester, St Helen (TL 9974 2538) Store house
This was possibly only ever a chapel rather than a parish church. There is much use of Roman bricks and tiles in evidence. Despite efforts to gain admittance, I have so far been unable.

Colchester, St Leonard (TM 013 247) Redundant
Mainly from the 15th century, some work from about 1300 still survives. There is an interesting hammerbeam roof in the nave. Civil War bullet holes can still be seen in the mediæval door.
Invested by the Church Conservation Trust. Key available nearby.

Colchester, St Mary at the Wall (TL 9925 2506) Arts Centre
This is known as the 'Humpty Dumpty' church by locals. The top third of the tower was blown off by Parliamentary forces during the siege of Colchester (1648). Concerts are held here, as are amateur dramatics. Open some Saturday mornings and on event days.

Dunton Wayletts, St Mary (TQ 6535 8832) Private residence
Rebuilt in 1876 in red brick, St Mary's retains much timberwork inside from the 15th century. It was converted into a house in the 1980s. The vestry is now used as a kitchen and the chancel as a living room. Iron gates and guard dogs faced me on my first visit - although the owners kindly allowed me into their home on a subsequent visit (the house was up for sale not long after this visit in 1993).

East Horndon, All Saints (TQ 6355 8953)   Redundant
The building you see today, of red brick from about 1500, is possibly the third church built on this site. Declared redundant in 1970, a campaign headed by Christopher Starr fought to save All Saints, which was finally vested in the Church Conservation Trust. Open by appointment with the key holder.

Frating, Dedication unknown (TM 0820 2235) Private residence
This has a Norman nave and a chancel dating from about 1300. It was much restored in the 19th century. The fine west tower was demolished in 1976, not long after which the church was declared redundant. Eventually it was converted to a house. A private residence not open to the casual visitor.

Great Clacton, St John the Baptist (TM 1770 1653) Redundant
This is a Norman church with a 14th century chancel and 15th century tower. I am unsure as to the future of this church. It lies redundant and is slowly decaying. The bulk of the town has shifted towards the seafront. Interior accessible only by appointment. Churchyard and exterior viewable at all times.

Langdon Hills, St Mary the Virgin & All Saints (TQ 6728 8635)  Private Residence
An early 16th century nave and chancel. Little has changed since its conversion to a house. It has a painted Charles II Royal Arms over the chancel arch. Churchyard accessible at most reasonable times. Interior only viewable with permission of occupant (he is a nice chap though!)

Latchingdon, St Michael (TQ 8877 9872) Private residence
On the main road through Latchingdon, St Michael's was converted into a house in the late 1970s. This small and compact church has lost its tower and chancel. It hints at having Norman foundations although the north wall is built in brick and clearly dated 1618. Now a private residence. The occupier is not happy to receive uninvited guests.

Lawling, Dedication unknown (c.TQ 900 015) Chapel demolished
It is believed that once there was a chapel beside Lawling Hall, which was ruined before 1650. Archbishop Lanfranc may have founded this chapel in the late 11th century. No visible remains. Apply to the Hall for permission to view the area.

Lee Chapel, dedication unknown (c.TQ 6921 8757) Lost Chapel
Until early in this century, remains of this ancient chapel were still visible on the outskirts of Basildon. It was sometimes called 'East Lee' but never appears to have been given parish status. It appears to have had an apsidal end. No remains are visible - site open at all times.

Little Bromley, St Mary the Virgin (TM 092 278) Redundant
A Norman nave, chancel from about 1300, a 16th century porch and a large 15th century tower greet you when you visit this fine church near the border with Suffolk. Invested by the Church Conservation Trust. Key available nearby.

Little Coggeshall, St Nicholas (TL 8538 2228) Redundant
This is mainly an early 13th century church with examples of some of the earliest mediæval bricks in its structures. It was originally part of Coggeshall Abbey, but after the dissolution of the Abbey became redundant and by the 18th century was being used as a barn. Key available from Coggeshall Rectory. Exterior viewable at all times.

Little Oakley, St Mary (TM 2121 2846) Private Residence
Declared redundant in 1973, this early 12th century church was converted into a house by the end of the decade. It includes a squat Tudor brick tower and some nice old doors and windows mainly from the 14th century. Not open to the general public.

Maldon, St Peter (TL 8508 0706) Thomas Plume's Library
One of three historic churches in Maldon, St Peter's was demolished in 1665 with the exception of the fine 13th century west tower. A number of social activities take place in the rebuilt nave, but the tower now houses a fine collection of antiquarian books donated by Thomas Plume to the town in 1704. Open: Tuesday, Wednesday & Thursday 2-4 pm and Saturday mornings 10 am till 12.

Milton (TQ 8716 8506?)  Vanished
I have often heard rumours of a church or chapel in Milton near Southend-on-Sea. There are reports that it was a religious building attached to the Priory at Prittlewell and that it sunk into the sea sometime between the 12th and 14th centuries. The town of Southend has since engulfed the hamlet of Milton. The sketchy references found do not make it clear whether it was a parish church or merely a chapel of ease. There are no references to what the structure looked like. Morant said that Milton had a "chancel or chapel of ease of which the remains were visible not long ago at low water mark." I have, however, yet to find any eye-witness reports. The exact location is unknown although it is believed to be on the Southend/Westcliff beach south of Milton Road.

Mucking, St John the Baptist (TQ 6853 8118) Private Residence
Originally of 13th century design, it was virtually rebuilt in 1852. It retains the original chancel and many of its outstanding features: sedilia, piscina and 13th and 14th century windows. In the past few years it has been declared redundant and has now been converted into a private dwelling. Not open to the public.

Netteswell, St Andrew (TL 4561 0935)  Study centre
Probably Norman and possibly even Saxon, this small church is now situated in the heart of Harlow New Town. It contains some nice glass and brasses and, since conversion, a great number of papers relating to the New Town. Open during weekdays for access to the records or to view the inside of the church.

Pattiswick, St Mary (TL 8168 2404) Private Residence
This picturesque little church has a 13th century nave, 14th century chancel and 15th century bell-turret. The nave includes a fine early 15th century roof. It has been tastefully converted into a house in the past decade. Not open to the public.

Romford 'Old church', (c.TQ 51 87) Demolished Chapel
Wright tells us that this chapel was built "some time after 1323" before which St Andrew's, Hornchurch, was where the inhabitants of Romford travelled to worship. The chapel stood "a quarter of a mile closer to Hornchurch" than the current church, in the area known as "Oldchurch." It was 28 ft shorter and 14 ft thinner than its replacement. Little else is known of this demolished chapel. Exact site unknown.

Shellow Bowells, SS Peter&Paul (TL 6160 0800) Private Residence
Rebuilt in red brick in 1754, this church has been converted into a dwelling in the last few years. Not open to the public.

Stansted Mountfitchet, St Mary (TL 521 242) Redundant
Extensively restored in the late 19th century this church retains much of interest. Two Norman doorways, a Norman chancel arch and a pair of fine 17th century monuments make this church well worth the visit. Invested by the Church Conservation Trust. Key available nearby.

Tolleshunt Knights, All Saints (TL 9269 1387) Greek Orthodox Church
Thought to date from the 12th century (by the thickness of the walls) this little church of just chancel and nave contains many details from the 15th century. Its greatest treasure is a stone effigy of a knight from about 1380 in full armour holding his heart in his hands. The church is closed but the key is available from the Greek Orthodox minister nearby.

Vange, All Saints (TQ 7151 8672) (closed at present)
Norman in origin this church was restored in 1837 by T Sneezum. It retains some attractive early features including a 12th century chancel arch, 15th century rood staircase and a Norman 'zigzag' decorated font. This church is now closed and its future does not look promising.

West Bergholt, St Mary (TL 9530 2808) Redundant
St Mary's consists of a nave, chancel, south aisle and west bell-turret. There is much evidence of 14th century work but Rodwell believes the nave and chancel are older. Of particular interest is the 18th century west gallery. Now invested in the Church Conservation Trust. If not open, the key is available nearby.

West Thurrock, St Clement (TQ 5929 7731) Owners: Proctor & Gamble
In the 12th century this church had a round nave (there is but one remaining in Essex - at Little Maplestead) but now consists of a square nave, chancel, tower, north and south aisles and chapels. Much of that which remains is from the 13th century but with a horizontally 'striped' tower of the 15th century. Its recent claim to fame is that it was featured in the film *Four Weddings and a Funeral*. Open by appointment only to the offices of Proctor & Gamble, West Thurrock.

West Tilbury, St James (TQ 6618 7771) Private residence
The chancel and nave are from the late 11th or early 12th century. A new west tower, north porch and vestry were added in 1879. It is now converted to a private dwelling. Not open to the public at any time.

Wicken Bonhunt, St Helen (TL 5114 3349) Chapel

The Chapel of St Helen is three quarters of a mile east of the parish church. Built in the 12th century it was restored in the following century and retains early windows. Owned by Bonhunt Farm - please request their permission before visiting.

Willingale Spain, St Andrew, (TL 5963 0731) Redundant

A delightful little Norman church set beside its neighbour St Christopher, Willingale Doe. Norman features survive in the windows and doorways. Redundant church - usually open.

Asheldam

Little Coggeshall

St Giles, Colchester

Tyrell Chapel, East Horndon

Willingale Spain

Chickney

Useful Addresses:

The Friends of Essex Churches
Sir Alastair Stewart
Walter's Cottage
North Hill
Little Baddow
Chelmsford
Essex CM3 4TQ
01245 222445

The Round Tower Churches Society
Mrs Lyn Stilgoe
Crabbe Hall
Burnham Market
King's Lynn
Norfolk PE31 8EN
01328 738237

The Churches Conservation Trust
Mr Richard Peck
89 Fleet Street
London EC4Y 1DH
020 7936 2285

English Heritage
Membership Department
Freepost 31 (W214)
London WIE 5EZ
020 7973 3434

The Friends of Friendless Churches
St Ann's Vestry Hall
2 Church Entry
London EC4V 5HB
020 7236 3934

Historic Churches Preservation Trust
Fulham Palace
London SW6 6EA
020 7736 3054

Chelmsford Diocesan Office
Guy Harlings
53 New Street
Chelmsford
Essex CM1 1AT
01245 266731

Royal Commission on Historical Monuments
National Monuments Record Centre
Great Western Village
Kemble Drive
Swindon
Wiltshire SN2 2GZ
01793 414700

Tolleshunt Knights

Frating

120

West Thurrock

Glossary of Architectural features

| | |
|---|---|
| 3-Decker Pulpit | Pulpit of three stages: Minister's pulpit with Clerk's stall and Reading Desk below. |
| Altarpiece | See Reredos. |
| Apse | Semi-circular end to the chancel, usually Norman. |
| Balusters | Small, usually circular, pillars. |
| Belfry | The church tower area where the bells were hung. |
| Brasses | Monumental plates of brass incorporating engravings of the deceased. |
| Buttress | Projection giving extra support and strength to walls. |
| Chancel | The eastern part of a church used by the church official. |
| Chantry chapel | Chapel connected with a monument in which masses were chanted. |
| Chapel | Chamber attached to a church in which an altar was placed. |
| Cinquefoil crocheted canopy | Intricately carved stone canopy with five leaves. |
| Clunch | A hard chalk used as building material. |
| Dormer Window | A window cut into a sloping roof and placed under a small gable or roof of its own. |
| Dripstone | Projecting moulding over doorways or windows used to throw off the rain or in some cases as ornaments. |
| Embattled | When a tower is finished with battlements. |
| Font | The vessel containing the consecrated water to be used in baptism. |
| Gable | Triangular shaped wall carrying the end of the roof |
| Gallery | A raised floor or stage in building. |
| Hammerbeam | Wooden beam used to strengthen the frame of a roof. |
| Hatchments | The Arms of the local gentry displayed on large tablets of wood. |
| Jamb | The side post of a window, door or chimney. |
| Kentish Ragstone | Hard coarse sedimentary stone that breaks into thick slabs - used as building material |
| Knapped Flints | Flints broken by hammering to disclose their more decorative interior |
| Lectern | A desk or stand usually holding the bible. |
| Limestone | Pale sedimentary rock used as building material |
| Memorial | An object to commemorate the deceased. |
| Mullions | The upright bars of stone, used to subdivide a window into one or more lights |
| Nave | The central avenue of a church or cathedral |
| Oratory | Small private chapel |
| Parapet | A breastwork or low wall used to protect the gutters and screen the roofs of buildings. |
| Pews | Seats in the nave used by the congregation |
| Piers | Pillars |
| Piscina | Shallow stone basin sited near the altar for use by the priest. |
| Porch | A small external structure to protect and ornament the doorway to a building. |
| Reredos | Wall or screen behind the altar usually ornamented. |

| | |
|---|---|
| Rood | Cross or crucifix usually placed below chancel arch. |
| Rood loft | Singing gallery above a rood screen. |
| Rood screen | Screen at the west end of the chancel where the rood was sited. |
| Rood stairs | Stairs giving access to the rood loft. |
| Sedilia | Three seats on the south side of the chancel used by priests |
| Shingles | Thin slabs of timber used on roofs and spires. |
| Spire | The steep and pointed roof of a tower. |
| Steeple | A tower and spire in combination |
| Stoup | Vessel for holy water sited near the main door |
| Tracery | Ornamental stonework formed by the curving and interlacing of bars of stone occupying the heads of windows |
| Turret | A small tower |
| Tuscan | Least ornamented architectural style |
| Tympanum | The filling in of the head of an arch. |
| Vault | An arched ceiling made of stone. |
| Vestry | Room attached to a church in which to keep vestments |

Architectural Styles:

| | |
|---|---|
| Saxon | 700 to 1050 |
| Norman | 1050 to late 12th century |

The Gothic Period is often divided thus:

| | |
|---|---|
| Early English | Late 12th to late 13th century |
| Decorated | Late 13th to mid 14th century |
| Perpendicular | Mid 14th to the mid 16th century |

However, the period 1145 to 1600 is sometimes divided otherwise:

| | |
|---|---|
| Transitional | 1145 to 1190 |
| Lancet | 1190 to 1245 |
| Geometrical | 1245 to 1315 |
| Flowing | 1315 to 1360 |
| Perpendicular | 1360 to 1500 |
| Tudor | 1500 to 1600 |

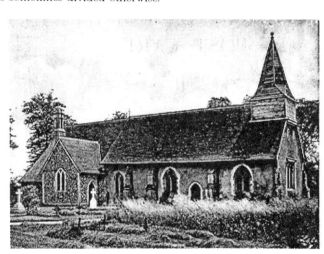

Pattiswick

Bibliography

Sources researched at the Essex Record Office

Essex Record Office, Parish Registers of Essex, ERO, 2nd ed 1993
Holman, Holman's MS Notes on Parish history TIP 195115
King, H W, Ecclesiae Essexienses TIP 19612-6
King, H W, Collectanea Historica et Topographica Spectantia Hundredo de Dengey in Comitatu Essexia a Henrico Guilielmo King
Rodwell, Warwick, Essex Churches - a wasting asset, Council for British Archæology, 1977
Royal Commission on Historical Monuments, Volume 1: North West Essex, 1916
Royal Commission on Historical Monuments, Volume 2: Central and South West Essex, 1921
Royal Commission on Historical Monuments, Volume 3: North East Essex, 1922
Royal Commission on Historical Monuments, Volume 4: South East Essex, 1923
Essex Archæology magazine, various
Essex Countryside, various
Essex Review, various

Essex books

'The Editor', Excursions through Essex (in 2 volumes), P.Youngman, 1819
Addison, William, Essex Worthies, Phillimore, 1973
Barret, C R B, Highways, Byways and Waterways of Essex Volume 1 & 2, Lawrence and Bullen, 1892 & 1893
Bax, Clifford, Highways and Byways of Essex, Macmillan, 1939
Benton & Jerram-Burrows, History of Rochford Hundred, various dates
Bertram, Jerome, Lost Brasses, David & Charles, 1976
Britton & Brayley, The Beauties of England and Wales: Vol 5 Essex, Unknown publisher, 1803
Buckler, George, Twenty Two Churches of Essex, Bell & Daldy, 1856
Collier, D W, The People's History of Essex, Meggy & Chalk, 1861
Cox, J Charles, Essex, Methuen, 1909 revised 1952
Cromwell, Thomas, History and description of the ancient town of Colchester (2 volumes), P.Youngman, 1825
Curtis, G C S, Redundant churches in Essex, County Planning Committee, 1976
Edwards, A C, A History of Essex, Phillimore, 1985
Haining, Peter, The Great English Earthquake, Hale, 1991
Hewett, C A, Church Carpentry, Phillimore, 1974
Hough, John, Essex Churches, Boydell Press, 1983
Jarvis, Stan, Hidden Essex, Countryside Books, 1989
Mee, Arthur, The King's England, Hodder & Stoughton, 1940
Morant, Philip, Morant's Essex (2 Volumes), 1730s
Pevsner, Nikolaus, The Buildings of England: Essex, Penguin, 1954
Phillips, Andrew, Ten Men and Colchester, Essex Record Office, 1985
Pusey, A Discovery of Old Essex, Hale 1985

Scarfe, Norman, A Shell Guide to Essex, Faber, 1975
Starr, Christopher, A Guide to Essex Churches, The Essex Churches Support Trust, 1980
Warren, C. Henry, The County Books: Essex, Hale, 1950
White, William, History, Gazetteer and Directory of Essex, Leader & Sons,1863


Books on Churches:


Appleby & Watkinson, The Parish Church of Saint Runwald, Colchester, Benham, 1942
Bailey, Brian, Churchyards of England and Wales, Magna Books, 1987
Bertram, Jerome, Brasses and Brass Rubbing in England, David & Charles, 1971
Bond, Francis, Fonts and Font Covers, Waterstone, 1895
Churches Conservation Trust, Visit Churches in Hertfordshire and Essex cared for by..., C.C.T,
1994
Cox & Ford, Parish Churches of England, Batsford, 1946
Crossley, F H, English Church Design 1040 to 1540 AD, Batsford, 1945
Cunnington, Pamela, How old is that church?, Marston House, 1993
Hall, P A & Tully, S A, St Margaret's church - Woodham Mortimer with Hazeleigh, 1991
Lane, Rev C Arthur, Illustrated notes on English Church History, Volumes I & II, Society for
Promoting Christian Knowledge. 1894
Maclear, Reverend G F The Village Church and What it Teaches, Society for Promoting
Christian Knowledge, 1893
Needham, A, How to Study an Old Church, Batsford, 1945
Parker, John Henry, A concise glossary of architectural terms, Republished by Senate, 1994
Smith & Poynter, Architecture: Gothic and Renaissance, Society for Promoting Christian
Knowledge, 1908
Spencer Stowell, H, How to Look at Old Churches, Methuen, 1925

St Peter ad Murum, 1900